THE
INTERFAITH FAMILY
GUIDEBOOK

Practical Advice for
Jewish and
Christian Partners

JOAN C. HAWXHURST

Dovetail
PUBLISHING

Kalamazoo, Michigan

To Mom and Dad,
in appreciation of the
spiritual and ethical foundation
you laid for me.

Acknowledgments

Since I first drove across the country in the summer of 1992, meeting with authors, clergy, social scientists and grassroots interfaith groups, a great many people have contributed to the genesis of our national organization dedicated to serving interfaith families. It is with great pleasure that I acknowledge the many people who have played a role in the creation and growth of *Dovetail*.

I am extremely grateful to the people who gave me their time, their ideas, their mailing lists and even their spare bedrooms on that first cross-country trip: Susan Gertz, Tina Giebisch and the New Haven interfaith group, Rabbi Steve Mason and the Hartford interfaith congregation, Dr. Egon Mayer, Lee F. Gruzen, Rev. John Wade Payne, Rabbi Roy A. Rosenberg, Father Peter K. Meehan, and Leslie Goodman-Malamuth. Without the support and encouragement of these people, I never would have begun this publishing project.

I will always be appreciative of the work of Saundra Heller, whose interfaith support group at Temple Emanuel in Denver was the catalyst for many of the early discussions between my husband and me, discussions that eventually led us to believe that couples such as ourselves could benefit from new kinds of resources.

I am grateful to the members, current and emeritus, of *Dovetail*'s editorial advisory board, all of whom have given freely of their time and talents: Rabbi Dr. Arthur Blecher, Nancy Nutting Cohen, Rabbi Irwin H. Fishbein, Leslie Goodman-Malamuth, Lee F. Gruzen, Father Peter K. Meehan, Father Dan Montalbano, Rev. Julie Parker, Rev. John Wade Payne, Rev. Dr. Bruce Robbins, Dr. Stanley Ned Rosenbaum, Rabbi Roy A. Rosenberg, Oscar A. Rosenbloom, and Dr. Andrew S. Watson.

I could never have survived the dual responsibilities of being both an editor and a new mom without the efforts of a fine and faithful associate editor, Mary Heléne Pottker Rosenbaum, whose insight and skill have sharpened and improved the journal immeasurably. As she prepares to take over the editing of *Dovetail*, I wish her all the best.

Without the creativity, pragmatism and dedication that Alison Siragusa has brought to the marketing of our resources, thousands of families would not know about Dovetail Publishing. And without her unflappable sense of humor, I would surely have given up and stomped away many times.

I am grateful to Alison and to Nancy Nutting Cohen for reading early chapters and offering helpful suggestions. I am indebted to Sandy Wachowski and the students at Western Michigan University who kept the office running while I wrote. And I am eternally appreciative of the support and devotion of my husband, Steve Bertman, who right now is juggling an energetic preschooler, a messy kitchen and a hungry infant on a rainy Sunday afternoon.

Finally, this book would not exist without the honesty and thoughtfulness of the couples and families who have shared their experiences and lives with us over the years of publishing *Dovetail*. Some consented to lengthy interviews, some wrote about their experiences, some shared their stories in interfaith groups. The rich lives of these women, men and children form the basis of this book.

Contents

Foreword

*At least one of the issues in the whole interfaith dilemma
is NOT whether individuals are being faithful to their
religions, but whether religions are being faithful to
their task of supporting people on their journey to God.*

Nancy Nutting Cohen

Whatever you think about Christians and Jews falling in love, marrying and having children, you will find food for thought in this book. Most likely you will see your opinion reflected here, too. And you are almost sure to discover at least a few pages that would be just right to give to so-and-so as a helpful resource.

One of the most remarkable features of **The Interfaith Family Guidebook** is its fair presentation of the many points of view on Jewish/Christian relationships and related issues. The author goes out of her way to respect and make clear the many voices and options that one now encounters. In most cases, she finds and quotes people who hold a great array of views, and includes stories of personal experience. This approach will surely help those who find themselves in the midst of one stage or another of such an intimate interfaith journey, if only by preparing them for the dizzying array of opinion and advice they are sure to encounter.

The order of the chapters is also helpful, following as it does the usual course of development of such a relationship. After an introduction, the book begins with the questions that arise as Jewish/Christian couples become serious enough about their relationships to consider marriage, and begin to confront the attitudes of family and religious institutions. It moves on to issues which the married couple will face, and then to questions regarding raising children, and on into the challenges that come at various life-stages.

Always the book gives readers the benefit of lots of first-hand experience, as well as available research and opinion. There is an excellent chapter on human resources, as well as an extremely helpful and up-to-date annotated bibliography. A very practical resource indeed!

As the product of my own parents' interfaith marriage and as a Presbyterian pastor, I believe that Christians and Jews would do well to devote more time to discussing the many realities and questions that come to focus and are lived through by those in interfaith relationships. All who want to support people living within, rather than apart from, our religiously diverse society need to talk more about how we can care for our people and communities. In particular, Christians who respect both the Jewish tradition and our own, and Christians and Jews who care about the ongoing vitality of the Jewish community, can ill afford to ignore the issues and those involved in them.

Christians and Jews do fall in love and marry and raise children. I hope that many of us will take advantage of **The Interfaith Family Guidebook** and make use of it not only as a resource for couples but also as a resource to animate discussions and dialogues in our local congregations and communities.

Rev. Dr. Jay T. Rock
Office of Interfaith Relations
National Council of Churches of Christ in the U.S.A.

CHAPTER ONE

Why Do You Need This Book?

When a Jew and a Christian make the decision to marry, they begin a journey of challenges and opportunities that will last a lifetime. Often interfaith couples feel isolated and alone in making these important decisions. Their religious institutions are sometimes silent, sometimes ill-equipped to help them navigate the practical issues they face.

If you can stand the stiff winds and strong waves associated with a sea change, it's an exciting time to be part of an interfaith family in the United States. While Jewish/Christian families are still faced regularly with negative responses from family and community, and while your path is still strewn with difficult decisions and uncomfortable discussions, you are beginning to attract the attention and interest of others who wish to observe and understand your unique situation. You are being taken quite seriously by researchers and granting agencies alike.

And with good reason. According to the most recent and reliable population studies, there are about one million Jewish/Christian couples in this country, and that number grows by about 40,000 each year. The national rate of interfaith marriage for Jews marrying today is 52 percent. In other words, more than half of the Jews getting married this year will marry people who aren't Jewish (and most of these partners will be Christians). It has been estimated that by the year 2030, there will be more children born of Jewish/Christian couples than children born of two Jewish parents.[1]

Despite their growing numbers, interfaith families have to look hard for information and help. When *Dovetail*, the national periodical for Jewish/Christian families, was founded in 1992, it was the first periodical to attempt to balance and respect the perspectives of both Jewish and Christian partners in interfaith marriages. For the first time, interfaith families could have up-to-date information delivered to their doorstep. In the tradition of *Dovetail*, this book will give you an opportunity to ask your own questions and share your own insights. And it will not condemn your decisions or take sides.

Is This Book for You?

Are you and your partner looking for insight and support from other Jewish/Christian couples? Are you trying to sort out conflicting emotions about your daughter or son's intermarriage? Would you like to hear about others who grew up in interfaith families? Do you wonder which holidays to celebrate with your children, and how to help them understand and appreciate both of your faiths? If you answered yes to any of these questions, then this book is for you.

These are some of the topics covered in this book:
• holiday explanations, traditions, and new ways of celebrating,
• programs—institutional and independent—for interfaith couples, their parents and kids,
• life-cycle events, such as marriage, birth, entrance into a religious community, and death,
• related family issues, such as how to deal with a mother-in-law or how to encourage family discussions,
• spiritual questions, such as how parents can understand their own evolving thoughts as they teach their children about God.

Communication is Key

Over and over again, you will hear from the experts and couples in this book that good communication is at the heart of every successful interfaith marriage. When two partners are able to share their feelings honestly and openly, and are willing to respect each other's differing outlooks, they are crossing the biggest hurdle facing them. When they are unable to be open and honest with one another, they are setting up roadblocks which will most likely trip them up in the future.

Susan Silverman LaDuca, Ph.D., a therapist and partner in an interfaith marriage, stresses the significance of building trust and open communication. "It is important for partners in a Jewish/Christian marriage to develop a trustworthy relationship which respects and acknowledges each partner's distinct religious and cultural heritage, regardless of which religion, if any, the couple chooses to observe."

"Regardless of how we view intermarriage," continues LaDuca, "we are witnessing a major shift in the culture of a significant population, with limited notice from educators, researchers, theologians, or policymakers. The increasing number of interfaith families has huge consequences in terms of cultural and religious identity for many Americans. What does it mean to be Jewish in America? What does it mean for a Christian to have a Jewish grandchild?"

The story of Tom and Nancy Hennick, of West Hartford, Connecticut, is typical of what happens to many interfaith couples today. "It all sounded so simple," remembers Tom. "After years of wandering through bachelorhood, I finally met the woman of my dreams. And what happens when two people meet and fall in love? They get married, of course.

"Did it matter that I was Jewish and my wife-to-be, Nancy, was not? Of course not. I am not a religious zealot and saw no problem sharing a life with someone who didn't share my religious beliefs. Nancy felt the same way.

"Until the children began to arrive. The truth is that conceptualizing something so significant and actually doing it are entirely separate matters. Literally, up to the minute my first daughter was born on August 21, 1985, there was no doubt in my mind that she and all Hennick babies would be Jewish.

"But Nancy had begun to have doubts. As the baby became more and more a reality and less a concept, she realized that her 'no problem' to Judaism was a problem indeed. She had been far more devout than I growing up. She went to church regularly and taught Sunday School. And as she thought more and more about separating herself from her beliefs, she began to have second thoughts."

The Hennicks face a very common dilemma: as long as they were a couple without children, their love for each other was enough to get them through any religious differences, but once their three children entered the picture, emotional attachments to each of their faiths of origin grew stronger and less pliable. "Suffice it to say," says Tom, "that our pre-baby vision—celebrate all religious holidays. from Rosh Hoshanah to Christmas to Passover to Easter complete with seders and Christmas trees, expose them to the best of both worlds and raise them as Jews—has undergone some serious revisions since Nancy began to have doubts and since we learned that she was not looked upon as the 'correct' person to raise Jewish children.

"Suffice it to say, too, that we are still struggling with our dilemma. Unfortunately, there is no rule book or how-to book when it comes to determining the religious course for the children of a mixed marriage. We considered a number of options. Although many of the options were valid, few seemed to work. Both of us put the cohesiveness and strength of our five-member family unit above all else. Nancy and I love each other very much and love our children more and more each day.

"But each time we try to resolve the religious dilemma with those basic precepts in mind, we run into our own religious upbringings, our own needs, and our own doubts about 'the right thing.'"

Couples like the Hennicks are struggling around the country with these difficult issues. Some, like Susan Gertz of Middletown, Ohio, find practical ways to help address the tangled questions of religious tradition and practice. Gertz is the author of **Hanukkah and Christmas at My House**, the first children's book to deal specifically and exclusively with life in an interfaith family.

"My cultural attachment to Judaism is very strong, and I want my children to experience that," says Gertz. "I want them to recognize and understand important symbols—the Torah, *sukkah*, menorah, seder plate—and feel that these things belong to them and are a part of their lives."

Her husband, Tom, was raised as a Presbyterian. "I don't regret having the experience, and I still hold many of the values," he says. "But I have broken away because I had a lot of trouble with the doctrine, the feeling that I was expected to believe that I'm right and you're wrong."

3

"Our personal beliefs are very similar," says Susan. "We both came away from our childhood experiences with a strong aversion to 'us versus them' religious views."

Susan's father is a cantor with a Reform congregation, and he has a Master's degree in family counseling. He had reservations about her marriage, wanting her to avoid the heartache and discomfort he thought would surely follow. Her marriage to Tom, Susan says, "was not within the scheme of how he imagined my life would be."

Over the years, though, her father has seen the very special family that Susan and Tom have created. He "sees the value in our family—he's come to appreciate as well as accept." Her mother "has been supportive all along, at the same time that she's been sensitive to my father's feelings."

Tom's mother, Mary Ellen, a practicing Presbyterian, lives with them and celebrates all the holidays, both Christian and Jewish, with them. She is visibly proud of her son and his wife.

Susan and Tom have two children. They are not enrolled in a Presbyterian or a Jewish religious school, because Susan and Tom do not want them to be taught a single "right" religion. Instead, the children attend religious school at the Unitarian fellowship in Dayton, where Susan and Tom are members.

"Faith is a personal matter," adds Susan. "Even in a single-faith household, you can't transmit religious beliefs to your children like genes for brown or blue eyes. Like all of us, they have to come to their own understanding by asking questions and making their own spiritual journey."

Susan and Tom mention several things when asked what helps make a successful interfaith marriage. First and foremost, they talk to each other, and to others, about their concerns and interests. They work hard to foster an open atmosphere of discussion and questioning in their home, so that they and their children feel good about asking questions.

Both Susan and Tom have come to terms with their feelings about the other's childhood religion. Over the years they have learned that preconceptions and prejudices left over from their upbringings can sometimes surface during holidays and religious observances. In these situations, honesty and understanding are key. "You may have no problem intellectually, but you can't just wipe out your feelings and your personal and cultural history."

Their home life does not focus exclusively on religious traditions. They share their common interest in science with the children. The whole family loves books and looks forward to a special reading time just before the children's bedtime.

"The most positive outcome of our interfaith marriage is that from the minute we decided to get married, everything has been a conscious decision. Every choice we make involves thinking and talking about our own beliefs."

Society's View of Interfaith Families

It's easy for interfaith families to get caught up in their own day-to-day experiences and solutions to the challenges they face. Couples often focus on sharing with each other and with supportive clergy. But it is also important to step back and look at how the general public views their situations. How are interfaith families seen and portrayed in the public eye?

In a representative sampling of media coverage, some recent coverage is of famous interfaith couples, like Michael J. Fox and Tracy Pollan, or couples with one famous partner, like Caroline Kennedy, Diana Ross, or Maria Cuomo. More is of everyday couples. Some coverage is matter-of-fact; some is skittish and oversimplified. Often it is clear that producers and editors are more concerned about creating a neat, presentable package than about exploring the complexities of life in an interfaith marriage. But TV networks, filmmakers, and newspapers are starting to pay attention to the fact that much of their audience is directly or indirectly touched by interfaith marriage.

When interfaith couples speak for themselves, they may be attacked for their views. When Marian Winik, a columnist for the *Austin* (TX) *Chronicle*, read a light, humorous piece about her own intermarriage on National Public Radio, the only responses aired were condemnations, one by a rabbi and one by a Jewish layperson, of her lack of understanding of the plight of the Jewish people. Although Winik privately reported a number of supportive responses and inquiries, no such support reached the radio waves. And the public outcry over the February 15, 1993, cover illustration of *The New Yorker*, which portrayed the interfaith (and interracial) embrace of a Hassidic Jewish man and an African-American woman, shows—among other things—that many still find interfaith relationships incomprehensible, even distasteful. Hopefully, the media will grow to play a positive public educational role, showing the realities, complexities, and normality of interfaith relationships.

Jonathan and Judith Pearl, founders and directors of the Jewish Televimages Resource Center (JTRC), have based their careers on studying, writing, lecturing, consulting and teaching about the image of Jewish themes and characters in popular television—what they have coined "Jewish televimages."

The Pearls suggest that intermarried or interdating couples are, and have been for some time, a regular part of TV fare. "But there is something new in television's recent portrayals of intermarriage, due to the changing societal landscape from which popular TV emerges, and which reflects and reveals a great deal about the evolving perceptions of intermarriage," write the Pearls. In TV's early "melting pot" years, young TV characters often blithely intermarried in order to assimilate, over the objections of their Old World parents. Scripts for these interfaith TV couples were written to show the similarities between Jews and Christians, and these couples lived happily ever after.

Today, on the other hand, TV viewers are presented with much more complex views of the interfaith marriage scenario. In the 1960s and 1970s, with the tremendous success of the miniseries *Roots* and the surge of ethnic pride, TV stopped trying to minimize the differences between Christians and Jews. Increasingly, viewers have seen popular TV characters who grapple with their religious identity, often within the context of an interfaith marriage. The manner in which TV interfaith couples celebrate holidays is one telling area of change in TV portrayals. "In many current shows," suggest the Pearls, "Hanukkah and Christmas—two wholly different and separate holidays—are no longer simplistically equated in a way that negates the distinctive religious and historical significance of each. By depicting the celebration of one holiday, without an obligatory and superficial nod to the other, television has come to acknowledge and respect the distinctiveness and unique spiritual messages of each."

"Intermarriage is an integral part of television as it is a part of life. By confronting the issue in all its dimensions rather than ignoring it, and by presenting increasingly realistic and varied approaches to interfaith romantic involvements, television gains respectability for its realism and sincerity, while viewers can surely benefit from the medium's maturing, refreshing, and encouraging new visions."[2]

Like television, the movie industry has explored the questions facing interfaith families. Leslie Friedman received her master's degree in Cinema Studies at New York University and is the daughter of an interfaith couple. She suggests that "of all the media of mass communication, film has provided the most accessible outlet for exploring issues of interfaith romance and marriage." Films such as Woody Allen's *Annie Hall* (1977), *A Stranger Among Us* (1992), directed by Sidney Lumet, and *When Harry Met Sally* (1990), all focus attention on the challenging aspects of interfaith relationships.

Friedman suggests that movies are perhaps ahead of real life when it comes to their treatment of interfaith families. "Intermarriage will never destroy religious values and tradition," believes Freidman, "as long as religion, in its infinite wisdom and compassion, is able to adapt to the times. Woody Allen is no less a Jew for falling in love with a Christian. But the Jewish community is less a community when it continues to disintegrate because it excludes. In a twist on the famous Groucho Marx line, it seems some Jews would rather not belong to a club that would not accept their loved ones as members."

When Jewish/Christian couples look for information and news about people in their situation, newspapers and magazines are often disappointing sources. Especially in the larger, more prestigious print media, intermarriage is almost always reported as a problematic factor contributing to the declining Jewish population, rather than as an exciting, potentially beneficial phenomenon. While such negative viewpoints are clearly held by many, the print media shows its bias and does its readers a disservice when it ignores more positive opinions on the issue of Jewish/Christian marriage.

Articles on the so-called December dilemma are perhaps the most frequent coverage granted to Jewish/Christian families. In recent years they have appeared in papers and magazines of all sizes and slants. A typical example is the December 1992 article in the Annapolis, Maryland paper, *The Capital*, which profiled a family that had decided to raise their toddler daughter as Jewish "to keep confusion to a minimum." The article included comments from a local rabbi who encouraged couples to raise children with a single religious identity.

In general, the press has a long way to go in digesting and conveying the complexities and myriad choices that are made with integrity and thoughtfulness by Jewish/Christian couples all over the country.

How Religious Institutions Respond to Interfaith Marriage

The amount and depth of media coverage of interfaith families is in many ways reflective of the amount of attention paid to this issue by society at large. As the numbers of interfaith couples in the United States rises, religious institutions, both Jewish and Christian, are taking another look at this phenomenon.

Christian Responses

Locally, Protestant ministers and Catholic priests in all but the most conservative denominations have come to accept the reality of interfaith families in their congregations. Since the percentage of Christians who marry outside the faith is miniscule, most Christian clergypeople do not feel that their faith tradition is threatened by a congregant's decision to marry outside the fold.

The Rev. Dr. Jay T. Rock, co-director of the Office of Interfaith Relations of the National Council of Churches of Christ in the U.S.A., and himself the adult child of an interfaith marriage, has considered the question of intermarriage from both a personal and professional perspective. Rock believes that the Christian community by and large has allowed the issue of interfaith marriage to be ignored or left invisible, and he advocates a more pro-active approach by Christian clergy. "For the sake of these couples and our communities, we cannot afford to avoid or prejudge the problems and possibilities presented by the increasing number of interfaith marriages. We need an approach that helps us all to engage the issues creatively, to see and discover without prejudice. Real human beings with specific needs, facing difficult challenges and bringing valuable gifts, deserve response from the Christian and the Jewish communities."

"In general, any child of an intermarriage raised as a Christian has been considered a Christian. Today, a Jewish partner in an interfaith relationship, or a

7

child of intermarriage, may hear an occasional anti-Semitic joke about the Jewish banker in the church social hall. But in a time of dwindling Jewish/Christian antagonism in the United States, those in interfaith relationships often can find themselves comfortably and creatively engaged in a Christian community."

Rock has observed, however, that interfaith couples will most likely find an absence of concern for their special problems, partly because of an assumption that anyone entering the Christian community leaves behind his or her former cultural identity. Church members often forget—or are never aware—that Christian symbols, rituals, and mores may be problematic or not readily accessible to Jews. It is assumed that somehow the non-Christian partner is as comfortable as the Christian partner is assumed to be.

Finally, posits Rock, "Christians have little awareness of the Jewish community's concerns about intermarriage. The Jewish concern for survival, its worry that it may finally disappear through assimilation, is surprisingly little known."

Christian institutions, being the vast religious majority in this country, have largely ignored the question of interfaith marriage. Most have done little or no formal study on the issue. An exception is the Presbyterian Church U.S.A., which has made great efforts to educate its clergypeople about interfaith marriage and to provide a welcoming atmosphere for intermarrying couples. The Presbyterians have produced a special guide for their members and ministers, which proclaims that "in the contemporary world, characterized by global interdependence and the daily interaction of people of differing cultures and religions, interfaith marriage may create networks of families never otherwise so related. . . . In this sense, intermarriage may tighten the web of the human family and the care, concern, and knowledge of people—God's people—in the global village. Interfaith marriage can provide an opportunity for growth and change."[3]

Jewish Responses

Unlike their Christian counterparts, Jewish institutions, many of whom see their survival threatened by rising rates of interfaith marriage, have devoted vast resources and energy to addressing this question.

Across the Jewish spectrum, there is a fair amount of agreement when it comes to sanctioning interfaith marriage by performing an interfaith wedding ceremony. The rabbinic guidelines for all four major Jewish denominations—Reform, Reconstructionist, Conservative and Orthodox—state that rabbis should not officiate at intermarriages. The Reform and Reconstructionist rabbinic organizations do not discipline those who digress. Nonetheless, the majority of rabbis feel that officiating at the weddings of interfaith couples suggests approval and is contrary to their understanding that Jewish weddings are to be performed only for Jews.

In a call for rational and concerned attention to needs of the growing number of interfaith couples, Rabbi Harold Kushner, author of **When Bad Things Happen to Good People**, says, "A generation ago, when a Jewish person married a non-Jew, it could usually be assumed that that person was on his or her way out of the Jewish community. Today we can no longer make that assumption. Interfaith marriages are far less likely to represent a rejection of one's faith and family, and far more likely to be the result of falling in love with a non-Jew in a society where 97% of our neighbors are not Jewish. In these new circumstances, there is a great need for mutual understanding."[4]

Kushner suggests that synagogues need to find ways of reaching out to interfaith couples, some of whom have felt rejection from their religious institutions in the past. He maintains that "interfaith couples should realize that their presence generates some strong and ambivalent feelings among even the most liberal rabbis and synagogue leaders. Couples need to accept that synagogues are not guilty of religious bigotry when they insist that certain rituals can be performed only by Jews. Memories of an unpleasant experience in one synagogue should not diminish an interfaith family's search for a communal setting in which to live out the Jewish part of their heritage."

With the ever-increasing number of interfaith families who want to affiliate with synagogues, Jewish leaders are being forced to rethink membership policies. Interfaith couples who seek temple involvement can be faced with painful realizations. A Christian father might learn as his son's bar mitzvah approaches that he may not stand on the *bima* with his child. Or a Christian woman may be asked to step down from her leadership role in a temple sisterhood when it is realized that the congregation's bylaws prohibit non-Jews from holding this position.

Says Dru Greenwood, director of the Reform movement's Outreach Commission: "We must continue actively to welcome the non-Jewish partner. This effort has to be balanced by the understanding that the synagogue is a Jewish institution, with its own integrity. Its challenge is to set appropriate boundaries and communicate them in a way that emphasizes inclusiveness rather than exclusiveness."

A 1991 survey by the Outreach Commission found that 88 percent of the temples who responded provided some form of membership for people who aren't Jewish. Eighty-seven percent allowed participation on all or most committees, but only 27 percent permitted non-Jews to serve as officers.

In the past several years, decisions related to interfaith marriage made by elements in the Jewish community have received widespread attention and sparked national controversy. The decision of Reform Judaism to limit religious school enrollment to children who are not being schooled in another religious tradition, and the decision of a Jewish newspaper in Connecticut not to print interfaith wedding announcements, have provoked strong emotions. These decisions raise issues within the institutions of the Jewish community and the larger debate prompted by them.

In December 1995, at its national convention in Atlanta, the Union of American Hebrew Congregations—the governing body of Reform Judaism, whose membership numbers about one million people in over eight hundred congregations across the United States—passed a resolution urging that Reform Jewish day schools and part-time school programs enroll only children not being schooled in another faith.

In part, the UAHC Religious Schools Enrollment Policy states: "We recognize that enrollment of children in a Jewish religious school is a complex decision that interfaith parents do not undertake lightly. It can have profound implications for the children, the couple and the household they have created and can entail significant sacrifice, particularly for the parent who is not Jewish. We respect the desire and acknowledge the challenge for interfaith parents to impart knowledge and appreciation of the heritage of both parents to their children, while giving them a singular and firm religious foundation on which to grow.

"Experience tells us that some interfaith couples who seek to enroll their children in Reform religious schools are not raising and educating their children exclusively as Jews. . . a path that we as committed Reform Jews cannot support.

"Therefore, [UAHC] resolves to . . . encourage congregations to . . . [offer] enrollment in Reform religious schools and day schools only to children who are not receiving formal religious education in any other religion, [and to] develop clear and sensitive procedures for communicating the goals of the school and enrollment policy to all parents, particularly interfaith parents."

The UAHC decision angered and frustrated many interfaith families. "It forces us away from the temple to find our own way," responded one reader of *Dovetail: A Journal by and for Jewish/Christian Families*. "I feel our children are less likely to choose Judaism when they are grown. It's also made it hard for my Jewish husband, who would very much like a temple bar mitzvah for our three boys."

Others think that the resolution may not be as harsh in practice as it sounds. "Our temple takes each family on a case-by-case basis," wrote a *Dovetail* reader, "and it will not necessarily follow the ruling." As this reader suggests, since the UAHC resolution is non-binding on member congregations, it is important to research what a local congregation has decided to do with respect to this issue.

The second decision that catalyzed national controversy about Jewish/Christian marriage was taken in July 1995 in Hartford, Connecticut. There *Jewish Ledger* editor Jonathan S. Tobin wrote an editorial arguing that a wedding between a Jew and a non-Jew was not an event for the Jewish community to celebrate, and therefore the *Ledger* would not print wedding and engagement announcements of interfaith couples. The editorial provoked dozens of strongly worded letters to the editor, both supportive and scathing, and prompted an editorial by William Safire in *The New York Times*, which took the debate nationwide.

Tobin was prompted to write the original *Ledger* editorial when he received a wedding announcement accompanied by a picture of a couple posed in front of a Christmas tree. He wrote, "I can't see into that young couple's hearts, but with such a picture, am I really supposed to think that they want to be part of an unbroken chain of Jewish life that will stretch to the future?" Tobin, dubbed "the Wedding Censor," later opined that "we are all voting on the Jewish future with our own behavior. Anyone has the right to vote 'no' or to vote 'I don't care,' but ... you shouldn't expect the rest of the Jewish community to cheer you."

All organizations, Jewish institutions included, are subject to the political pulls and attachment to the status quo that come from being created by human beings with strong wills and differing visions. And, as noted above, different local temples—and national Jewish organizations—are handling these issues in different ways. In trying to cope with interfaith marriage, Judaism is struggling with an extremely delicate and difficult issue, to which there are no easy solutions. Interfaith families can watch and wait with frustration, disappointment, and maybe some hope for the future of American Judaism. You can turn away from the Jewish community altogether. Or you can enter into the debate, involving yourselves in your local temples even when you feel shunned or belittled, because your commitment to the tradition of your Jewish partners is stronger than your distaste for the current state of affairs. Each of these choices is a valid option, and interfaith families will have to make this choice for themselves.

Syncretism and Interfaith Dialogue

Many Jewish/Christian couples consider their relationships to be a microcosm of interfaith relations, a showcase of what can happen if different religions learn to live with each other. There is much validity in this. A successful Jewish/Christian family engages in interfaith dialogue on a daily basis. From grappling with difficult religious differences with a spouse, to choosing elements of religious education for children, to explaining traditions to a neighbor, the day-to-day business of life in a Jewish/Christian family makes us experts at interfaith dialogue.

Interfaith couples—by necessity—accomplish the difficult task of expanding beyond our cultural and religious traditions in order to understand someone different. We are forced to make ourselves vulnerable by risking to share deeply-held religious beliefs. This task is often excruciatingly difficult, even with someone we know and love.

Despite these difficulties, we benefit enormously from such dialogue. By moving beyond our trepidation and sharing our different life experiences, we can reach out and form connections and relationships, replacing mistrust and misunderstanding with respect and visions for our shared future.

It is important for interfaith couples, at the same time that they enter into dialogue and visions for a shared future embracing both of their faith traditions, to be wary of the dangers of syncretism. Religious scholars and clergypeople agree that religious syncretism detracts from the meaning and autonomy of both faiths. While their histories are doubtless intertwined, Christianity and Judaism each exist as independent and vital traditions, and their separateness should not be ignored. An interfaith couple runs the danger of syncretizing, or combining, Christianity and Judaism when it places Hanukkah decorations on a Christmas tree and dubs it a "holiday tree," or when it teaches children that the two faiths are interchangeable save for differing opinions on Jesus.

Rabbi Tirzah Firestone, a spiritual leader in the Jewish Renewal movement and herself the former partner in an interfaith marriage, has strong feelings on the issue of syncretism. "In our marriages and in our communities, it is much easier at times to merge, to blend. And on small points, like how to pour the wine or to say amen, it may be better to do so. But on issues of one's uniqueness, personal or religious, I ask myself, can we afford to blend? It may be more harmonious in the short run, but the cost may be a loss of soul. I prefer to use as a model the image of a perforated boundary, a semi-permeable membrane which allows for lots of exchange, confluence, and interaction, yet always with the permission to retain each of our individual identities."

The question of syncretism is, of course, a delicate one for interfaith couples who are working to include both faiths in their family and community life. Says Rabbi Roy Rosenberg, co-author of **Happily Intermarried: Authoritative Advice for a Joyous Jewish-Christian Marriage**, who has worked extensively with interfaith couples: "I do not envision, nor do I advocate, a 'syncretism,' a combination of the two religions, but I do see a time when a loving acceptance of Jews by Christians, and of Christians by Jews, will take place, for both communities constitute 'God's people.' This process, though it might occur without intermarriage, will be hastened by the large number of interreligious families. If a husband, wife and children can live together in mutual respect and love, so, too, can the religious communities. This is a lesson that interreligious marriage will be able to teach."

Rabbi Rosenberg realizes that, just as it is essential in a Jewish/Christian home, dialogue is vital between local Jewish and Christian congregations and national institutions. The challenges and benefits of sharing our experiences and beliefs are similar whether the sharing is done by two individuals, two congregations, or two national groups. And, when dialogue occurs at one of these three levels, it affects attitudes and actions at the other levels as well.

For example, an important step toward society's understanding and acceptance of Jewish/Christian couples is sharing between Christian and Jewish communities. If, through increased communication and shared programming, members of local Christian congregations can get to know and feel comfortable with members of nearby Jewish congregations, and vice versa, then perhaps it would be easier for people of both faiths to understand and relate to couples in their neighborhoods who have chosen to intermarry and maintain ties with both communities. Likewise, if the individuals at national institutions like the U.S. Catholic Conference or the American Jewish Committee can learn more about each other, that learning might influence their decisions about policy and programming for families.

Perhaps the current efforts at interfaith dialogue, manifested in many ways and at many levels across the country, will contribute to an increased understanding and acceptance of the choices made by interfaith couples.

Jewish/Christian couples looking for signs of interfaith cooperation and dialogue in their own neighborhoods can turn to a number of different institutions. In some communities, Jewish and Christian congregations already come together for annual Thanksgiving services, Holocaust observances and Passover seder celebrations. Other communities have ongoing interfaith study groups and town-wide interfaith councils capable of making joint decisions and releasing joint statements on current issues. Some interfaith groups cooperate to provide shared social ministries, like soup kitchens or homeless shelters.

Jewish/Christian couples should see the importance of such cooperation and work to promote it in their own communities. Interfaith families are in a unique position to serve as bridges between their faiths of origin. Daria Donnelly, a Christian married to a Jew, recognizes the importance and the difficulty of her own involvement in interfaith dialogue: "I am more needful of the dialogue and I also understand that a marriage such as ours is at the center of controversy in the dialogue. . . . Yet I believe that our experience has something to say to the scholarly debate."

There are many ways to begin a local-level Jewish/Christian dialogue in your community. You might try encouraging two local congregations to jointly sponsor a shared celebration or worship service that would bring together Jews and Christians who might not otherwise come in contact. Or you might start an ongoing dialogue group through your church and/or synagogue. Consider approaching your public library or community college about sponsoring a series of programs on local cultural and religious differences. Or contact one of the growing number of interfaith support groups for help in finding a local starting point.[5]

No matter which kind of approach your community takes to interfaith dialogue, the important thing is for Christians and Jews to meet each other and share their experiences. Such sharing will be beneficial to interfaith families, local religious communities, and national religious institutions, as well as to society at large. Look around locally for religious and secular groups and organizations that might help Jews and Christians in your neighborhood to begin talking.

CHAPTER TWO

Should You Consider Marriage?

Y ou've met a wonderful person and fallen in love. Your future looks bright and clear. Of course you realize that you have real religious differences, but with careful discussion, you think that you can live with them. You imagine building a home together where both of your faiths are respected and understood. Then, when you proudly announce to the world your intention to marry, brows furrow among your family and friends.

Why are so many people set against your marriage? What should you expect for the rest of your engagement? Can you in fact make the compromises and commitments necessary for a successful interfaith marriage? As you are no doubt already aware, there are serious challenges and opportunities facing an interfaith couple considering marriage, and there are no shortage of opinions on whether or not you can make a go of it.

In the words of clinical psychologists Ann and Milton Matz (he is also a rabbi; together they co-direct the Pastoral Psychology Institute at Case-Western Reserve University School of Medicine), "As it is with all families, the important question [for interfaith partners] is not whether there are any disagreements, but whether the disagreements are being negotiated successfully."

As you begin the process of learning about one another, do not avoid the tough questions and the disagreements. Instead, show your partner how much you love and trust him or her by opening up about these deeply personal issues. You might choose to use the following list of questions to help you get started:

- What are your goals in life?
- What are the values you hold most important?
- What aspects of your partner's character do you most cherish, and why?
- What is important to you about your religion?
- Describe your image of God.
- Do you and your family agree on your religious beliefs?
- What do you know about your partner's religion? Are there elements of his/her religious beliefs that you disagree with or find unacceptable?
- What do you see as the cultural differences between the two of you? (Specifics might include money, tastes, family and in-laws, child-rearing, food and sexuality, among others.)
- How do you envision the family that you and your partner will create?
- What does your extended family mean to you? How do you feel when you visit your partner's family?
- Have you talked about children? How will you raise them? What religious training, if any, will you give them?

- What are some of the issues on which you've already discovered disagreement? How will you negotiate these? Are there any which cannot be resolved?
- What attracts you to your partner?
- What does marriage mean to you?
- What does it mean to be someone's life partner?

Confronting Your Differences

As a Jew and a Christian, the two of you have much in common. Your faiths are grounded in a common message. Says Rabbi Irving Greenberg, co-founder of the National Jewish Center for Learning and Leadership: "From the time that Judaism and Christianity grew together, matured into separate religions, and separated, until today, the two have had one central message in common: the triumph of life. Both affirm that this is a world grounded in (or created by) God, an infinite source of life, goodness and power."

But, as you have no doubt already found, you also have many differences. There are the obvious theological and religious issues around Jesus as the Messiah and the Jews as the chosen people. There are differences in holidays and worship styles. And there are often deep cultural and ethnic clashes.

Unlike most North American Christians, Jewish Americans make a distinction between being culturally Jewish and being religiously Jewish. Of course, those who are religiously Jewish are also culturally Jewish. But many modern Jews consider themselves culturally, but not religiously, Jewish—that is, they don't attend synagogue regularly, they don't keep kosher, and so on. However, in the United States one never hears a Christian making a distinction between being culturally and religiously Christian!

For both Christians and Jews, ethnic background is yet another layer of consideration. On the East and West Coasts of the United States, for instance, distinctions are made between the Roman Catholic Church and the Irish Catholic Church. Similarly, Jewish people's ancestors came from such diverse countries as Russia, Poland, and Spain. Each of these cultures has its own identity and its own way of living its religious beliefs. You each need to understand your own and learn about your partner's cultural, ethnic, and religious identities.

An interfaith couple swirling in the American melting pot has to confront substantial cultural differences as well. Historically, Christianity has often attempted to separate itself from culture, focusing instead on a direct, transcendent relationship with God. Judaism, on the other hand, depends heavily on culture and melds it with religion into a resilient way of life.

Thus, when making decisions about their joint lifestyle, Jewish/Christian couples must grapple with two very particular cultural attitudes. Sometimes it's difficult to see how two people with such different backgrounds can approach a shared decision. Whether the decision is about what to name a baby, how to celebrate a holiday, or where to bury a parent, Jewish and Christian traditions can seem to be steaming toward each other down a potential collision course.

Collaboration is possible: Jewish and Christian partners can work together to create a harmonious home, in many different ways, and with many different results. A family might decide to celebrate one partner's faith while respecting the other's faith, or it might incorporate both faiths into the family's routine— either way, both partners' cultural ties can be respected and appreciated.

In some ways, being part of an interfaith family is like living in a foreign culture. Your partner may do things in ways you've never even considered. Strange and disturbing cultural differences can even lead to culture shock. In a handy little paperback called **Survival Kit for Overseas Living**, L. Robert Kohls offers lessons that can apply as much to interfaith couples as to people planning to work or study overseas.

Culture shock, says Kohls, comes "from the experience of encountering ways of doing, organizing, perceiving or valuing things which are different from yours and which threaten your basic, unconscious belief that your enculturated customs, assumptions, values and behaviors are 'right'. . . . It builds up slowly, from a series of small events which are difficult to identify." Sound familiar?

Kohls sees that cultural differences become more apparent and disturbing after an initial "honeymoon" period. Initial euphoria is followed by irritation and hostility, then by gradual adjustment. Finally, one learns to adapt, becoming "bicultural."

Jewish/Christian couples can develop tools to help them deal with cultural differences. Perhaps the most important skills to help in coping with culture shock are a sense of humor, realistic goal-setting, and an ability to tolerate and learn from failure. Development of these three traits will go far in ensuring an interfaith family's successful adventure in this country's cultural melting pot.

Can It Be Successful? Opinions from Clergy

As institutional concern swells with the numbers of interfaith couples, the topic of interfaith marriage takes an increasingly prominent position in national religious and interreligious debate. As interfaith couples consider whether or not they can create a home together, they often are exposed to the opinions and guidance of clergypeople.

As an engaged interfaith couple, you'll certainly get mixed messages from the religious community, but at least there are channels of communication. After years of silence or guarded policy statements, people in the religious community are finally talking openly about intermarriage. At the 13th Annual National Workshop on Christian-Jewish Relations, held in Pittsburgh in November 1992, and again in October 1996, at the 15th National Workshop in Stamford, Connecticut, panel discussions directly addressed the issue of interfaith marriage. Conservative Rabbi Stephen Steindel gave one well-known opinion: "From a traditional Jewish perspective, from the orientation of almost every rabbi in America, interfaith marriage is fraught with dangers."

But his view was not the only one. Another panelist, the Rev. Robert L. Brashear, a Presbyterian minister, is himself a partner in an interfaith marriage. "People who have made the decision to intermarry have made that decision out of their own integrity," he asserted. "We as couples no longer feel apologetic. In fact, we would like to feel respected. All too often we feel that we are characterized by, on the one hand, having made a misinformed, tragic choice, for which we will be tolerated, or being somehow involved in the willful destruction of the Jewish people on the other hand. Neither of these things feels very good."

On a second panel, Rabbi Sanford Seltzer, Director of Interreligious Affairs for the Union of American Hebrew Congregations (Reform Jewish congregations), made the following observation: "Fifty years ago, the incidence of Protestants marrying Catholics was hardly acceptable in either faith community, and the incidence of Christians marrying Jews was considered virtually anathema to both groups. Obviously, things have changed radically."

Yes, things have changed radically, and will continue to change. Following are a variety of reflections gleaned from Jewish, Protestant, and Catholic clergy.

A Conservative Rabbi

Rabbi Joshua Hammerman is the Senior Rabbi at Temple Beth El in Stamford, Connecticut. He also serves as the president of the local Council of Churches and Synagogues. "I am a Conservative rabbi; I will not perform intermarriages. I agree with and believe in the official stance of the Conservative movement on intermarriage point by point. I've tried to live in a real world, and when it comes to intermarriage, there is no more real issue for most American Jews.

"In some specific cases in my congregation, a couple's intermarriage has nothing to do with a lack of Jewish identity or a lack of affection toward the religion. In some cases, it really is a matter of falling in love, strange as it might seem. But they have fallen in love with something other than the religion which I espouse. So there is tension there, because the couple feels guilty about approaching me. . . . I will immediately meet with them, to clarify the issues and help them figure out the best way for them to proceed. Even if I cannot perform their ceremony, I will reach out with as much warmth as I can, so that they will continue to think of the synagogue as a possible place for them to raise their children."

A Reconstructionist Rabbi

Rabbi Emily Korzenik is rabbi of the Fellowship for Jewish Learning in Stamford, Connecticut. "It must be understood that intermarriage is a survival issue for the Jewish people. It behooves us to respond to it in a positive and productive way. Inclusivity rather than exclusivity is not only more gracious and more generous, it is also more responsive to the needs of Jewish survival. There is much we can do. The Jewish family must offer a practicing and welcoming Jewish home. Increasingly, Reform and Reconstructionist congregations are receiving the non-Jewish spouse as members of their congregations.

A Presbyterian Minister

The Rev. Dr. Jay T. Rock, co-director of the Office of Interfaith Relations of the National Council of Churches of Christ in the U.S.A., asks, "Is it possible to hold Judaism and Christianity together in the life of a relationship? I think this is the wrong question. The pivotal issues are not those of compatibility of religious traditions, but those raised by the sensitivities and conduct of the people involved. A better question would be, can a Jew and a Christian together fashion a relationship that gives spiritual life to themselves, their children and their communities? Many Christians and Jews are engaged day-to-day in living out a variety of answers to this question."

A Congregational Pastor

The Rev. Gary Brown is Senior Pastor of the First Congregational Church in Stamford, Connecticut. He is also past president of the Council of Churches and Synagogues of Southwestern Connecticut. In his words, "Marriage is not a sacrament in our church. Each local congregation runs its own show, and therefore the pastor has the responsibility of making choices as to whether and when to marry a couple.

"Many people who come from different backgrounds are actually more thoughtful about the religious dimensions of their lives. At the same time, there can be a lack of religiousness, a lack of understanding of their faith, whatever it may be; however, the same is true of marriages where both people are from Protestant backgrounds. It is my belief that a person's faith cannot be fully nurtured simply on an individual basis, that we need a community of faith in which to nurture our faith.

"While I understand the motivation of those who are attempting to draw the lines carefully and to keep integrity in what they're doing as leaders of religious communities, I have taken another approach. I put myself and my training and experience at the service of those who come to me wishing to live healthy and strong lives as husband and wife, despite differences in their religious backgrounds."

A Catholic Priest

The Rev. Richard Futie is the pastor of St. Mary's Roman Catholic Church, in Stamford, Connecticut, and has a JCL degree (Licentiate in Canon Law). "In the Catholic tradition, we have seven sacraments, and marriage is one of them. Marriage has been ordained by God, and it has the ability to give grace to those who receive it.

"The church recognizes, for the good of society, the validity of all marriages, to Catholics, to Jews, to Protestants, to Buddhists, etc. But when a mix occurs, for the good of the individuals and the faith that they treasure, a careful look has to be taken as to how, from the Catholic standpoint, what one believes will be preserved and propagated.

"The church asks the two partners to come to the priest, as well as to the rabbi, to discuss what needs to be respected and honored during the course of their being joined together. For the Catholic, this would involve a dispensation by the ordinary—the bishop or cardinal—of the diocese. The dispensation can only be granted by him, with the understanding that the Catholic will respect the non-Catholic's conscience and need to practice his or her religious belief. It is understood that Catholic parties will do all in their power to preserve their own practice of their faith and to share that faith with their children."

Insights from Successful Interfaith Families

Despite the admonitions and ignorance of many segments of the religious commmunity, interfaith couples are getting married in increasing numbers. Interfaith couples often see themselves not as problems but as examples of progress in interfaith dialogue and understanding.

Lee F. Gruzen, author of the valuable book, **Raising Your Jewish/Christian Child,** has wrestled with the questions facing interfaith couples for two decades. She believes that couples must embrace their cultural and religious differences and enjoy the learning that follows. "My husband and I both value our own backgrounds and treasure what we learn about each other's religious and ethnic heritage. We honor our Jewish and Christian roots—each culture is important, and we are unwilling to forfeit either of them.

"Contrary to myth, the differences aren't cause for divorce, but as in all marriages, they're reason for thoughtful discussion, argument, negotiation, and growth." Gruzen cites the work of sociologist Egon Mayer, who has made a career of studying interfaith couples on behalf of the Jewish community. In his

1985 book, **Love and Tradition,** Mayer noticed how often the couples he inter-viewed reported surprise and shock when their differences began appearing for the first time. During their courtships the lovers had reveled in their commonality and the great shared areas of their lives. But suddenly the smallest detail took on enormous emotional significance, and a gulf appeared between them that had never existed before. "And couples never become so accustomed to each other that the differences stop surfacing," says Gruzen. "Every life cycle reveals a new foundation of ethnic conditioning, and it's a life's work to understand what dif-ferences can mean and how to deal with them. Fortunately, the task becomes easier with practice."

With time and experience, an interfaith couple can develop enough trust in its love and likemindedness to accept the inevitable differences and allow them to enrich their lives. Often partners agree to disagree, and in so doing, are con-tinually reminded how much they truly have in common.

"Contrary to the tradition that maintains that interfaith differences only lead to trouble and alienation," says Gruzen, "I've found that they're a compelling, vital presence, continually viewed through one's evolving knowledge and emo-tions. They can challenge a person's identity on the deepest, most mysterious levels. But they can also flatter and entertain, inspire and guide, and illuminate one's own power and beauty. They can draw people out of themselves and help them reach out to become their richer and wiser selves."

Another partner in an interfaith marriage, Lisa DiCerto Tischler, who has written for Catholic publications about her experiences, remembers back to the beginning of her relationship. "The first time I ever attended a Jewish service was with John on Rosh Hoshanah. I will never forget the feeling of warmth and spirituality that washed over me when, during a prayer, John put his *tallis*, the blue and white prayer shawl, around both of us. I felt as prayerful then as I do in my own church. Not only do I enjoy learning about Judaism, but I have also felt a resurgence of love for my own faith. The stories and lessons of my childhood are still dear to me, and maybe even more respected when I try to teach them to John. He agrees. It's as if in being teachers to each other, we have learned again to appreciate our own heritages.

"We live in a world that does not often look favorably on interfaith couples. Too many people see us as a threat to organized religion, or as examples of a lax moral upbringing. Both of us consider ourselves to be very respectful and thought-ful on the subject of faith. I never thought about Catholicism as much as I have since I met John. His questions about my religion forced me to think through concepts I had accepted blindly before."[1] DiCerto Tischler and her husband rely on their friends and family in interfaith relationships for support and guidance as they navigate the questions of their family life.

Tirzah Firestone, a rabbi in the Jewish Renewal movement in Colorado,

21

saw her marriage to a Christian man as "a grand experiment, an experiment in learning to balance amongst the paradoxes." She noted the delicate balancing act between tradition and new consciousness. "I am pulled by the voices of the past, who accuse me of lack of commitment to tradition and history.

"On the other side, I am pulled by the voices of the future, who support my desire to achieve a new level of consciousness. What we are doing in our household and our community is new to human history. It presages a new covenant between peoples and between faiths, and I feel blessed to go forward and offer encouragement to others who struggle with the experiment."

And for Ralph Gonichelis, pastor of a Congregational church in Connecticut, the theological and practical challenges of being married to a Jewish woman have helped him and his wife to broaden their horizons and increase their appreciation for diversity. "After more than sixteen years together, we believe that interfaith marriage, particularly involving clergy, is a healthy way to promote interfaith understanding. We hope to model a relationship of openness and empathy between a practicing Jew and a committed Christian, despite the centuries of suspicion between our two peoples. We even hope that in some small way our marriage, by working well, is bringing about justice, peace and *tikkun olam* (repair of the world)."

How Can Interfaith Couples Talk About Jesus?

As they navigate the balancing act that is an interfaith relationship, Jewish and Christian partners alike must eventually face one of the most critical questions for an interfaith couple: how does each partner view Jesus? The answer to this question will figure heavily in the degree of compatibility the couple enjoys, and perhaps even to the success or failure of their relationship.

"Regardless of what anyone may personally think or believe about him," writes Jaroslav Pelikan, noted Yale theologian and historian, "Jesus of Nazareth has been the dominant figure in the history of Western culture for almost twenty centuries." How can a Jewish/Christian couple talk about and respect each other's feelings about a man who has come to mean so much—and so many different things—to the Western world?

In many instances, both partners in a Jewish/Christian relationship have emotional and deeply-held beliefs about Jesus. For Christians, Jesus is the foundation of their faith. For many Jews, he symbolizes centuries of persecution and marginalization.

Yet, in order for a Christian and a Jew to consider marriage, they must almost always test and stretch the beliefs with which they were raised. Christians who plan to spend their lives with a Jew must be able to reconcile their own religious belief in Jesus with their emotional commitment to a partner who does not worship Jesus as Lord. And Jews who intermarry must be able to respect someone who venerates a man whom their tradition teaches was not the Messiah.

Says Rabbi Roy Rosenberg: "On the Christian side, the name or identity of the Messiah possesses tremendous importance. During most of Christian history it was taught that anyone who refused to acknowledge Jesus as the Messiah sent by God was not eligible for the fullness of salvation that God had prepared for the righteous. Plainly, a Christian who subscribes to this ancient conviction should not marry a Jew (unless that Jew embraces Christianity). To be 'happily intermarried,' a Christian must be able to accept Jesus as his or her Messiah but allow the Jewish partner to retain his or her beliefs about this complex theological issue."[2]

Interfaith couples trying to talk about Jesus can benefit from the new wealth of scholarship on the historical Jesus. Recent works by prominent theologians and historians show that many of the words and actions that the Gospels attribute to Jesus were actually added by his followers after his death. These scholars have reconsidered Christianity's teachings in the light of discoveries about what Jesus actually said and did. And it appears that much of the Christian theology that is troubling to Jews is not based on Jesus' actual teachings. Jesus was, in the words of DePaul University theologian John Dominic Crossan, a "Mediterranean Jewish peasant cynic" who announced the possibility of "religious and economic egalitarianism," the "brokerless kingdom of God." Jesus lived and died as a believing, albeit radical, Jew. He did not claim divinity for himself; rather, it was claimed for him by the earliest Christians. This new interpretation of Jesus' teachings helps many interfaith couples begin to see their differing beliefs with a fresh perspective.

Whether we are Christian or Jewish, many of our ideas about Jesus were instilled in us during our childhoods. According to therapist and researcher Joel Crohn, author of **Mixed Matches: How to Create Successful Interracial, Interethnic, and Interfaith Relationships**, "many people end their formal religious training in early adolescence. Although they may be very sophisticated in most aspects of their lives, their vocabulary for talking about religion is often very limited."

Often, once interfaith couples begin to talk about what they actually believe about Jesus, as opposed to what they've been taught in Sunday school or at the dinner table, they find that their religious beliefs are much closer than they imagined. But getting to the point of actually feeling comfortable talking about this emotionally charged issue is a major step.

Crohn has found that interfaith couples who openly discuss their religious differences form stronger bonds than those who don't. And Rabbi Steven Carr Reuben, author of **Making Interfaith Marriage Work**, cites as "the single most common interfaith problem" that many couples don't know how to talk to one another about religion. "Learning to communicate effectively and supportively about religion is, I believe, one of the most important skills you can ever learn," he writes.

A Rabbi Shares His Insights

Dr. Arthur Blecher, a rabbi and psychotherapist in Washington, DC, has counseled hundreds of interfaith couples. His doctoral work focused on the theological, communal and psychological implications of marriages between Christians and Jews, and he has considered in detail the question of how interfaith couples see Jesus within the larger framework of a family's religious life. He writes that, "Religious family life for interfaith couples (and indeed for many same-faith couples as well) often is limited to the observance of some ceremonies and folk customs and the teaching of basic ethical values to the children. The reason for this religious thinness may be that interfaith couples seek common, safe ground for family religious life, avoiding deeper spiritual inquiry and substantive religious dialogue.

"I believe interfaith families—no less than same-faith households—should be free to bring the full richness of spiritual exploration and religious dialogue into their homes. For Jewish/Christian couples who have agreed that the Christian partner's heritage is to be part of family life, Jesus must be included in the exchange. Yet I know of few interfaith couples among the hundreds I have worked with over the years who talk much about Jesus. In fact, some couples report to me that they find trying to discuss Jesus to be both confusing and distancing.

"How can interfaith families talk together about Jesus? I believe the key is to distinguish between the teachings *of* Jesus and the teachings *about* Jesus.

"First of all, it must be understood that a Jew who accepts Christianity's assertion about the divinity or the kingship of Jesus is deemed to have crossed the borderline between Judaism and Christianity. However, in my opinion, learning about the life of Jesus, reading the statements attributed to him in the New Testament, or giving consideration to Jesus' philosophical teachings, in no way constitute a conversionary process. It can only add to the richness of a couple's life if the Jewish partner (and maybe the Christian partner as well) learns about Jesus' life and is familiar with the basic Christian doctrines about Jesus. I can know what is on the other side of the fence without jumping over that fence. The important point for Jews in relationships with Christians is that learning about the teachings of Jesus does not necessarily mean crossing the boundary line between Judaism and Christianity—nor does admiring the life of Jesus, nor even does being inspired by those of his statements that may resonate.

"Nonetheless, partners in interfaith relationships need to be aware that the majority of the Jewish community is quite defensive about Jesus. This defensiveness is the direct result of Christianity's intrinsic evangelism. Most Jews probably would view with suspicion (or even condemnation) any individual Jew who is in any way interested in anything about Jesus. So ingrained is Judaism's silence about Jesus, that a Jew who expresses admiration of his life will be suspected of flirting with Christianity, and a Jew who quotes Jesus' statements in a sympathetic way might be viewed as a heretic. I believe this is both unfair and theologically unfounded, but it is a sociological fact of life.

"The challenge for interfaith households is to transmit substantive religious heritage and not reduce it to the mere sampling of isolated pieces of religion or folk culture. Religious nourishment for interfaith families requires a lot more thought and substance than that. I think the fundamental key to success in this endeavor is the same as all other aspects of intimate relationships: self-awareness, mutual respect and the commitment to care for each other."

Couples Share Their Experiences on the "Jesus Question"

The question of how to discuss Jesus in an interfaith family is an intensely personal and emotional one. Each Jewish/Christian couple will come up with its own unique way of dealing with its different perceptions of him. Most couples agree that they cannot avoid the issue, and that they prefer to discuss their differing ideas about Jesus rather than remaining silent.

For Karen and Dan, the subject of how to talk about Jesus comes up more frequently now that they have a young daughter. Karen, raised in a large Catholic family, acknowledges that "we need to decide how to present to Katie this person who was Jesus."

"We haven't really sat down and said, 'Let's talk about Jesus now,'" continues Karen. "I think that we will focus on Jesus' life and not his death. Whether he's God or not—who knows for sure? The most important aspect of Jesus for us is his example—the parables he told and the values he espoused. I know that we will talk about Jesus with Katie. I don't want to pretend with her that he didn't exist, or deny my belief in him. But my Christian belief has evolved to focus on the way that Jesus lived his life, rather than concern about his resurrection and our salvation. The words and actions of Jesus are a model for our ethical behavior. I want Katie to learn about and follow the example that Jesus, like other prophets, gave us."

Dan, who comes from an observant Jewish family, agrees. "The contribution that Jesus made was major and profound. In a sense, Jesus was killed for his beliefs, like Martin Luther King Jr., or, more recently, Yitzak Rabin. All of these people were challenging the status quo, trying to bring about radical change, and they were intensely disliked and finally killed for their actions.

"I see celebrating Christmas," he continues, "like celebrating Martin Luther

25

King's birthday. There are important human lessons to be learned from the lives of these great men, and we can all—Christian and Jew—certainly appreciate the moral and ethical imperatives that they preached. As I think about teaching our daughter, I know that the lessons of Jesus, along with Judaism's ethical teachings, will be an important part of what we pass on to her."

Dan admits that he still has some trouble with the idea of talking about Jesus. "After growing up learning that anything not Jewish is not kosher, I still have moments when I'm working to come to terms with my own background. On the one hand, I will be vigilant in teaching Katie about the historical periods when Jews were oppressed in the name of Jesus. On the other hand, I have to remind myself that I can talk about Jesus in a positive way and not betray my upbringing. I have not yet totally let go of that discomfort, but the more I talk about Jesus, the less I'm threatened by him. And whenever I get beyond the historical oppression and the childhood admonitions against him, I can see the valuable lessons he can teach all of us, regardless of what we believe about his divinity."

"In our family, questions are all still open for discussion," Karen concludes. "We don't have any set rules for what we must believe," concurs Dan. "If Karen wanted Jesus to be the major spiritual force in our family, it would be threatening to me. Luckily, our beliefs about Jesus the man fit together nicely."

Dan and Karen really are lucky. Sometimes two partners' ideas about Jesus cannot be reconciled. In his book **Making Interfaith Marriage Work**, rabbi and counselor Steven Carr Reuben describes the situation of John and Melony. The couple has "discovered that although they agree on much when it comes to religious observance, and both feel that they share certain religious values, there is one issue over which they seriously disagree.

"John has discovered that his belief in Jesus is a very important part of his life. It is a constant frustration and source of separation between them that Melony, as a Jew, doesn't share that belief. Each holiday becomes filled with tension as they both bend over backward not to offend the other with their various religious symbols and rituals.

"As adults they can resolve relatively painlessly, for most adults are able to choose to be tolerant of another's right to believe whatever he or she chooses. But, when it comes to children, to the many decisions regarding what they feel is important to pass on to the next generation, they run into a theological brick wall.

"Neither of them will be happy if *their* child is taught the theology of the other. Neither would be satisfied to place the religious upbringing of their child in the hands of the other. It is so painfully clear to them that this dilemma has no solution that they are resigned to an exclusively adult relationship, knowing that when they do want to have children, they will both want it to be with someone whose beliefs are consistent with their own."[3] John and Melony have been forced to accept that their differing beliefs about Jesus may someday drive them apart.

Most interfaith couples, however, have an easier time reaching consensus than do John and Melony. For Ted and Mary, the specific question of how they talk about Jesus in their family has not been a primary focus. Mary, who describes herself as "the more verbal one," says that she and Ted "talked about it before we got married, when we decided to raise our children with both faiths." Raised in a Roman Catholic family, she "still believes strongly in what she was raised with," although her church attendance is sporadic. More important to her than church attendance, she says, "is that our kids grow up with the knowledge of what it means to live a good life. Jesus as a prophet, even without the God connection, still offers an example of how to be decent and kind and to do the right thing, and I want our two daughters to learn from his example."

"I believe in one God," says Mary. "Jews and Christians both pray to one God. I know they say that Jesus is supposed to be the Son of God, but I have no problem with thinking of him as a prophet. I know my mother would be shocked to hear me say that. She is pretty clear about telling us that our kids should be raised with religion, and preferably the Christian one."

Mary's husband Ted was raised in a somewhat secular Jewish family, where there was no formal religious training and "Jesus wasn't praised or belittled." Ted "used to feel uncomfortable in church services," but has become more relaxed about attending during holidays.

"It is important to me that our daughters are exposed to the things I was exposed to as I grew up—the stories and lessons that Judaism teaches. But it is also important to me that they learn about Mary's background, and that includes Jesus."

Asked how he would feel if his daughters decided that they believed in Jesus as Saviour, Ted replied that he "wouldn't be overjoyed or broken-hearted, neither devastated nor excited." And Mary agreed, when asked about her feelings if her daughters rejected Jesus. "I don't think it would bother me as long as they turn out to be happy, well-adjusted, good people."

"So many other things in our lives have been really easy," Ted muses. " We get along well with each other's families. We're all healthy. We don't have financial problems. So I guess this is the one area of our lives that is not an easy thing."

"In some ways," summarizes Mary, "I'd put Ted above my religion. And that is what will get us through the hard questions."

CHAPTER THREE

How Can You Pull Off a Wedding?

After months of learning about each other's traditions, endless discussions of all the practical issues with extended family and friends, and lots of soul searching, you've made the decision—you're going to get married. You are concerned about the content of your wedding ceremony, and you want your families' two traditions to be respected and included in your own special and unique ceremony. But even the earliest signs are that planning your wedding will be challenging. Your mother calls your wedding canopy a rose trellis, his mother calls it a huppah. You want a full Catholic Mass, but then you remember that his family won't be allowed to take communion. He'd like to include a recitation of the traditional Jewish wedding blessings, but you're afraid your family will be put off by the Hebrew. Your local pastor has agreed to officiate at your wedding, but she has no experience with the Jewish traditions you'd like to include.

What are the special issues facing you as you plan your interfaith wedding? Where can you turn for advice, support, and examples? What can you learn from interfaith couples who can look back on their own wedding days?

Partners planning an interfaith wedding will be challenged to find representatives of their two religious heritages who are willing to perform their wedding ceremony. You will be challenged to bring together two sets of closely-followed traditions with-out unduly upsetting either family. Most importantly, you will be challenged to create together a ceremony that expresses your commonly held values about marriage, family, and community within the context of two different religious traditions.

You can create a wedding ceremony that is a wonderful, meaningful ritual for you, your extended families, and your guests. In this decade of exploding openness, as more and more people reach across religious and cultural barriers to choose a mate, wedding ceremonies are changing too. Couples are looking to include more spiritual meaning in their wedding rituals. A January 1996 survey conducted by *Modern Bride* magazine found that 85 percent of all engaged couples choose to have a religious ceremony, as opposed to a civil ceremony. Very few couples, interfaith or not, simply take what their chosen officiant offers them in terms of a ceremony—couples want to be involved in making their wedding ceremony something that is personally meaningful to them.

Making the Most of Your Engagement

As you and your partner become involved in designing your own wedding service, you can spend a great deal of time and energy learning, not only about the beliefs and traditions with which each of you were raised, but also about each other's values, dreams, and goals. Carve out some time to think together about the meanings of the ritual you are about to share. For interfaith couples, this time is crucial, for each of you brings a different and deeply felt set of traditions and beliefs which must somehow be brought together, in a wedding ceremony and in a shared life.

Here are some questions to get you started:

- What do you want to communicate about your relationship through your wedding ceremony?
- Do you want a formal or informal ceremony? Religious or secular? If religious, what does that mean to each of you: a specific denomination's ceremonial structure? non-denominational? spiritual, but without mention of God?
- How important is it to have a representative from each of your religious traditions present at your ceremony? participating in some way in your ceremony? leading your ceremony? Why is this important?
- What traditions, if any, from each of your religions and cultures do you want to include? How does the Christian partner feel about there being Hebrew in the ceremony? How does the Jewish partner feel about the name of Jesus being mentioned in the ceremony?
- How will each of your families participate?

As you begin to create your own wonderful ceremony, you will learn valuable lessons about each other, lessons which will last long after the rings are exchanged and the rice is thrown. These lessons are important, and you should take advantage of those who can help you as you learn them. If the person you ask to officiate at your wedding offers premarital counseling, take her or him up on it. If your officiant doesn't offer such counseling, find someone—a professional counselor or therapist—who will spend several sessions with you and your partner, probing the difficult issues you'll face as an interfaith family. You'll want to talk openly with your partner about everything from money matters (you may be surprised at how differently two people can look at this question!) to how you'll raise your children. If you can't find a local source for premarital counseling on your own, call the American Association of Pastoral Counselors at (703) 385-6967 for a referral in your area.

This premarital exploration is vital to a successful interfaith marriage. As you begin to share with your partner, you may find you have a hard time expressing the details of your religious background. You're not alone. Most of us are never pressed to talk about what our faith means and why. Most of us hesitate to discuss our own beliefs for fear of damaging the precious relationship we are nurturing. But if you don't talk about what you believe now, it will come back to haunt you in the years to come. So, if you find that you can't tell him why you feel you have to have a priest bless your rings, or if she just can't understand why the huppah is so important to your vision of your wedding day, seek out resources that can help both of you understand your respective religions.

You can also learn from the experiences of others. Well before your wedding day, seek out other couples who have been happily intermarried for at least five years. Of course, interfaith couples can help you with the details of your wedding, but don't stop there. Talk to interfaith couples who have children. Ask them about how they've dealt with their religious and cultural differences. Ask them about the difficult decisions they've made about home life and education. The advice and insight such experienced interfaith couples can provide will help you and your partner grow together long after your wedding day.[1]

While it is easy to get caught up in planning a wedding ceremony, which seems to represent all of a couple's values and concerns, it is important to remember that, after that half-hour ceremony is over, you'll start a much longer lifetime together. The most important preparation, says Maury Kopman, the Jewish partner in an interfaith marriage, is to be sure that you are getting married for the right reasons. "Make sure you really love the other person," he says. "No matter what adversities you come up against, if you know deep down that you really want to marry each other, anything can be worked out."

Finding An Officiant

When you and your partner decide to get married, one of the first hurdles you'll face as an interfaith couple—and potentially one of the hardest to surmount—is the choice of an officiant for your wedding ceremony. Especially if the Jewish partner feels strongly about having a rabbi take part in the wedding ceremony, you should prepare yourselves for an emotional search.

What to Expect When You Ask a Minister

From the Christian community, by and large, you'll receive a supportive response. Interfaith marriage has become an accepted (although not advocated) reality in all but the most conservative denominations, and announcement of your engagement may well be met with little or no resistance from your Christian pastor. Some interfaith couples even feel that the challenges of their special situation are invisible to clergy. On the other hand, a minister or priest may ask you some tough questions and may insist on thorough premarital counseling. No matter what the initial response from the Christian officiant you approach, he or she will almost certainly consent to being part of your wedding ceremony.

That's not to say that you won't have to do a little prodding. For Catholics, this may mean helping clear Church obstacles, like paperwork and dispensations, out of the way. Catholics who wish their interfaith wedding to be binding in the eyes of their church must request a special dispensation. Father Peter

Meehan, a Catholic priest in Manhattan and co-author of **Happily Intermarried: Authoritative Advice for a Joyous Jewish-Christian Marriage**, suggests you visit your local parish priest armed with knowledge. "Your official parish, where you have the right to be married, is where you live now—even if you haven't been going there regularly. All official things have to be channelled through it. Your parish is not where you were born, the city where you are to be married, or where your mother lives, or at the university where your cousin the priest works. It is where you live.

"All priests in the world can assist at an interfaith marriage, if they're official," continues Father Meehan. "If necessary, they can do the paperwork to make themselves official. And if all the proper papers are filed, a priest does not even have to be present for a wedding to be officially recognized by the Catholic Church. (This was not the practice 25 years ago.) So when you go to the rectory door, instead of looking for a priest to marry you, look instead for someone who will help your wedding to be officially recognized and who will be able to assist in making preparations that reflect your spiritual values."

What to Expect When You Ask a Rabbi

Expect a very different response if you decide to approach a rabbi about participating in your wedding. Even if you ask your family's long-time rabbi, he or she may well refuse your request. While it may be difficult to see past the hurt this causes, try not to take your rabbi's decision personally. It is part of a much bigger—and very complex—issue. The majority of the Jewish community, as we saw in Chapter Two, sees interfaith marriage as a danger to be avoided.

In 1995 the Rabbinic Center for Research and Counseling in Westfield, New Jersey, sent a detailed questionnaire to 1,794 Reform and Reconstructionist rabbis across the country. Of this number, 334 rabbis, or 47 percent of the rabbis who responded, said that they officiated at intermarriages under certain specified conditions. Thirty-nine percent do not officiate but are willing to refer to rabbis who do, and 14 percent neither officiate nor refer. Furthermore, data collected in this survey suggest "that the number of rabbis who refer to other rabbis is increasing and that significantly fewer rabbis require, as a condition of officiating, that children be raised as Jews or that the rabbi be the only officiant."[2]

One important point for you and your partner to clarify before looking for a rabbi is this: do you both want a Jewish and a Christian officiant at your wedding, or would you be satisfied with a rabbi as the sole officiant? This question is important for you to answer, because only a few rabbis will co-officiate with a Christian clergyperson. More rabbis will officiate on their own at a "Jewish-style" interfaith wedding—where there is a wedding canopy and Hebrew blessings, but the marriage contract is a civil one rather than a ketubah—but often only if you promise to raise your children as Jews.

32

Interfaith marriage is the most hotly debated issue for American Judaism today, and it is worthwhile to learn about why, especially if you'd really like to have a Jewish representative at your wedding. Following are the very different opinions of three rabbis on the topic of interfaith wedding ceremonies.

A Conservative Rabbi

Rabbi Barry Baron serves Congregation Beth Am, in Houston, Texas. He does not officiate at interfaith wedding ceremonies. "My goal is to assist everyone who comes into my congregation in furthering his or her spiritual development. My welcome, and my congregation's, is the same for interfaith couples as for all others: come and join us in belonging, growing, learning and believing in a God who stands for us, cares about us, calls us to a covenantal relationship, and asks us to work for the perfection of creation. Notwithstanding this welcome, I do refuse to officiate at interfaith marriages. Jewish law sanctions the marriage of Jews to each other, and, as a rabbi, I feel that I can only officiate at marriages which Jewish law sanctions.

"My love for Judaism stops me from officiating at interfaith marriages even as it leads me to reach out and embrace interfaith couples. There are many other rabbis in the United States who substantially share my views on these issues. Our stance does not please everyone. Many people have told me that I cannot expect interfaith couples to feel welcome after marriage if I send them away at the point of marriage. I cannot answer this assertion directly. I can only say that the force of tradition which leads me that way is the same force for deeper spirituality and meaning in my life and the lives of others, including many who are in interfaith marriages."

A Reconstructionist Rabbi

Rabbi Emily Korzenik leads the Fellowship for Jewish Learning in Stamford, Connecticut. She will officiate at a Jewish/Christian wedding if the couple is committed to raising Jewish children. "In general the leaders of the Jewish community have been exclusive when we should be inclusive. Too often we have been rejecting, although rejection is always bruising and almost always futile. Indeed, rabbis do not claim that their refusal to participate in wedding ceremonies is preventive. They are acting from conviction and/or according to the rules. The rabbinic guidelines for all denominations state that rabbis should not officiate at intermarriages. The Reform and Reconstructionist rabbinic organizations do not discipline those who digress. In any case, the majority of rabbis feel that participation at the weddings of interfaith couples would suggest approval and be contrary to their understanding that Jewish ceremonies are to be performed only for Jews.

"But rabbis must be receptive from the beginning. We cannot turn people away, then 'grudgingly' accept the couple after the fact, and expect that there will be no scars, no residue of resentment. Granting that our attitudes are born of millennia of persecution and fear for our survival, these rejecting attitudes are neither gracious nor productive. In his most recent study of intermarriage, socioligist Egon Mayer presents statistics indicating that it makes no difference whether or not rabbis officiate at interfaith weddings. It is not simply that more rabbis should perform wedding ceremonies. The rabbis must give time and effort to create bonds and establish expectations.

"One thing is sure: when a caring Jew and an uncommitted nominal Christian marry, there is a real likelihood that a sturdy Jewish family will emerge. Why should we not make every effort to encourage and assure that eventuality?"

A Reform Rabbi

Rabbi Charles Familant is a marriage and family counselor in the California Bay Area and co-leader of a local interfaith community. He frequently officiates at interfaith weddings. "Rabbis who perform intermarriages in this country are still very much in the minority, and they have no standard requirements. Some rabbis require attendance of classes in Judaism prior to the wedding. Others want assurances that the children will be raised as Jews. Still others require premarital counseling.

"Premarital counseling is my sole requirement, whether or not both parties are Jewish. My chief concern is that, as responsible adults, a couple is capable of resolving issues in a manner which enhances the marriage.

"When people turn to me for assistance, they have almost always already made a decision. To decline their request does not prevent their marriage but, in the case of the Jewish partners, denies them the opportunity to reconnect with their Jewish roots, often after years of estrangement. In the case of the non-Jewish partners, opposition to intermarriage leaves the impression that rabbis and Judaism are discriminatory and devoid of compassion, thus destroying any incentive for further learning.

"Jews marrying non-Jews often become more keenly aware of their Jewish identity than might have been the case if they had married Jews. They request books on Judaism and attend workshops on Jewish practice. It is not a foregone conclusion that intermarriage necessarily leads to the loss of Jewish identity, either of the Jewish partner or of the offspring.

"Discussions on intermarriage tend to overlook the fact that the partners have an enormous amount in common. Some, after years of dating people from their own religious and cultural backgrounds, have discovered in their chosen mate a far deeper bond, in comparison with which cultural and religious similarities seem quite minor."

If, after reading these three rabbis' opinions, you feel very committed to having a Jewish presence at your wedding ceremony, ask yourselves why. Do you feel the need to demonstrate your ongoing commitment to Judaism to the Jewish side of the family? Do you feel the need to "balance" a Jewish influence against the Christian elements of the ceremony you are planning? Do you feel drawn to Jewish wedding traditions, like standing under a huppah and breaking a glass? Some of these reasons can be satisfied without a rabbi as co-officiant at your ceremony. Perhaps you could ask your local rabbi, not for his presence at your ceremony, but for help with writing the Jewish portions. You can probably include traditional Jewish elements, like the huppah, some traditional Hebrew blessings, and the broken glass, without a rabbinical presence—just ask your officiant. In some areas, you may even be able to find a Jewish justice of the peace to perform your ceremony.

If you still feel that you'd like to have a rabbi co-officiate at your wedding, it probably can be done. Ask around—chances are that other interfaith couples in your area have already done a search for sympathetic local rabbis. If you can't find interfaith couples on your own, read through the society pages of your local newspaper, noting the weddings performed by both a rabbi and a minister or the names of couples who are likely interfaith (like McCarthy and Goldberg). If you can track them down, call these newlyweds for more information on their officiants.

Be forewarned: a few rabbis who co-officiate at interfaith weddings, especially those who advertise, can demand large fees for their services while providing little guidance and support before or after your wedding day. You may be faced with the choice of paying a lot of money for someone who is not very helpful to you, or not having a rabbi at your wedding. If you are contacting a rabbi you've found in an advertisement, ask in a tactful way if you may speak with other couples they've married, and then find out from these couples how much help they received.

You may find an out-of-town rabbi willing to come to you, but again, be prepared to pay hefty fees and all travel-related expenses. (Just for the sake of comparison, according to **Modern Bride** magazine, the average cost of a formal wedding in 1995 was $17,634, of which $273 went to fees for clergy, church, or synagogue.)

Of course, most rabbis are not going to officiate at your wedding for the money. There are rabbis who legitimately want to reach out to interfaith couples, usually because they see this as a way to show couples that they are welcome in the Jewish community.

Make Your Best Choice

Your wedding is a celebration, and when approached mindfully and with the intent to engage the participation of everyone present, your wedding ceremony can become a meaningful ritual. Choose your officiants carefully, making sure that they're committed to focusing on the two of you and your guests as the prime reasons and focus for your celebration.

By the day of your wedding, if not sooner, you should be secure and relaxed in the knowledge of what your wedding ritual and celebration will entail—the events and significances of each stage of the ceremony; your officiants' ability to comfortably and joyously lead you, your wedding party, and your guests with clarity and purpose. You should feel that all details of the ritual are being taken care of by your officiants, allowing the two of you to focus on being connected to one another in your heart and your spirit.

Couples have widely differing experiences with the officiants they choose. A Protestant woman from Oklahoma married her Jewish fiancé in her grandmother's home. Looking back, she wishes that she had incorporated more religious traditions, both Christian and Jewish, into the ceremony. "It was cold, even though the justice of the peace was good." The couple had been unable to find a rabbi willing to officiate at their ceremony, and although their minister was willing to participate, the couple decided that having only Christian clergy representation was not fair to the Jewish family. If she had it to do over, she would "find someone to represent both sides and make it more meaningful."

A Catholic woman from northern Virginia remembers her disappointment that the priest who co-officiated at her wedding ceremony was not more supportive. The rabbi, she wrote, was the best part of the ceremony—"everyone loved him," but the priest was there "under duress." He was 30 minutes late for the ceremony, and she was afraid he wouldn't show. If she had it to do over, she would "seek out a sympathetic priest while we were still dating."

Sometimes the act of officiating for the first time at an interfaith wedding can affect the clergy involved, giving new insight into the challenges and opportunities faced by a Jewish/Christian couple. For the Rev. David Matthew, a Presbyterian pastor in Oregon, the impression he later shared with his congregation was strong. "When a young couple, Jew and Christian, came to me and asked to be married, I had my doubts. And I'm sure Helen's rabbi had his doubts. Should I have said, "Don't do it"? Should I have said, "Listen, you are of two different faiths, and you will always feel an incredible tension"?

"I wish all of you could have been there, on that cool summer day three months ago, out in an open field in the Clackamas River Valley, to stand where I stood, to see what I saw: Sitting under the same sky were Jews and Christians, together. Singing a wedding song from a Jewish story were a coalition of two church choirs. And standing together under a Jewish canopy were a Christian man and a Jewish woman—both called by God, both gifted by God, both irrevocably loved by God, and now both becoming one flesh together, like a wild olive branch and a cultivated olive branch being grafted to the same holy tree."

You and your partner may not find an officiant like Reverend Matthew, and you may find that choosing an officiant is the most difficult part of planning your wedding. While you are in the middle of this decision, you may feel hopeless about getting what you want, and one or both of you may end up compromising your original ideas about who would lead your ceremony. But remember that once you've chosen the officiant for your wedding, you'll be able to move on to the exciting task of planning your ceremony. And no matter who officiates, you can still create a meaningful, inspiring service that communicates your goals and dreams as an interfaith couple.

Options for Your Ceremony

When it comes to planning their wedding ceremony, some couples choose to be married by representatives of both of their faiths in a combined service. Other couples avoid the interfaith obstacles by choosing a civil ceremony, by choosing one religious ceremony over the other, or by planning two separate services (one the actual wedding, the other a blessing of the marriage). Still others choose an all-embracing alternative like the Unitarian Universalist Church. Following are the basic choices for your wedding ceremony. Most interfaith couples choose one of the first two options.

1.　Choose one religious tradition.

If only one partner feels strongly about his or her religious identity, you can choose to have a wedding in only that tradition—either a Jewish wedding or a Christian wedding. In this case, you will need to find a representative of only one of your faith traditions. By choosing to have either a Jewish or a Christian ceremony, you will bypass many of the objections raised by clergy about interfaith weddings, so it should be easier to find an officiant. And sometimes, an officiant in this position will graciously agree to include elements from the other partner's tradition. A Catholic priest or Protestant minister will probably be willing to let you break a glass at the end of the ceremony or stand beneath a wedding canopy. And sometimes a rabbi or cantor will allow a reading or a song from the Christian tradition (although no mention of Jesus would be appropriate).

Be aware, however, that the partner who chooses not to include his or her own religious tradition in the wedding ceremony may later regret or resent this decision. If you decide to go this route, make sure that you think through, as individuals and as a couple, what this decision means for your life together after your wedding day. Are you deciding that you will celebrate only one religion as a family? Are you deciding about possible conversion of the partner whose faith is not represented in the ceremony? How will each of you feel if the uncommitted partner experiences a renewed interest in his or her religious tradition after you are married?

If you choose not to include your own traditions in the ceremony, do not keep that decision from your parents. Fill them in on the content of your ceremony in advance, so that they are not stunned on the day of the wedding.

2. Balance both religious traditions.

If you are both committed to your individual religious traditions, you can choose to have a representative from each of your faith traditions at your wedding ceremony. This is one of the most difficult, and yet most popular, choices made by interfaith couples.

In most parts of the country, it is not easy to find a rabbi willing to co-officiate with a Christian minister in such a ceremony. In some large metropolitan areas, however, Christian and Jewish clergy who have teamed up in support of interfaith families actually end up developing strong relationships with each other and with the community of intermarried families in their area. In metro areas like Washington DC, Chicago, and San Francisco, Jewish/Christian clergy teams are available to help interfaith couples with their weddings, as well as with religious rituals later in life, like baby namings and coming-of-age ceremonies.

If you are able to find both a Jewish and a Christian officiant willing to work together, you will almost always discover that the search was well worth the effort. Intermarried couples who spend the time and energy to create a ceremony which incorporates what is important to each partner from their respective religious traditions usually feel that their ceremony is the most memorable part of their wedding day. And most clergy who consent to co-officiating at an interfaith ceremony are very helpful when it comes to selecting readings, scripture and rituals that come together in a meaningful, inspirational ceremony.

3. Have two ceremonies.

If you are both committed to your individual religious traditions but cannot find clergy willing to co-officiate, you can schedule two separate ceremonies. Only one will be legally binding, so the second ceremony is technically a blessing of the marriage. A rabbi who is not willing to officiate at your full-blown, legally binding wedding ceremony may be willing to bless your marriage afterwards in a smaller ceremony, perhaps at the site of the reception. Or a small civil ceremony with a Jewish flavor might be followed by a religious Catholic (or

Protestant) ceremony. These alternatives may be a diplomatic way to maintain the separation between your two religious heritages while helping both partners—and both families—to feel respected and included.

4.   Find a "neutral" religious tradition.

Some interfaith couples choose to be married in the Unitarian Universalist Church, or the Ethical Culture Society, because these traditions are inclusive and embracing of both Jewish and Christian beliefs. A couple can have a traditional, yet neutral, non-denominational ceremony.

5.   Have a civil ceremony.

If your religious traditions are not central to your vision of your wedding day, you can avoid some religious difficulties by having a civil service with a judge or a justice of the peace. Some civil officiants are even willing to include simple religious traditions or readings in their standard ceremony. Be aware that you may lose the pomp and circumstance of a religious wedding.

6.   Conduct your own wedding ceremony.

You can have a private legal service, in a judge's chambers or at a mayor's office, with only yourselves and perhaps close friends or family as witnesses. Once the legal aspect of your marriage is complete, you can have free rein over a larger public ceremony of your own design and leadership. You can combine whatever elements of your two traditions you desire, and choose whomever you want to preside over the ceremony. In fact, in some states it is now possible to marry yourselves lawfully without a legally sanctioned officiant—you can officiate at your own wedding! When you are inviting guests to a ceremony that is neither religiously nor legally binding, it may be seen as courteous for you to tactfully inform them of this (so that they don't feel "cheated out of the real thing").

Ideas From Couples Who Have Been Through It

Couples who have gone through the experience of an interfaith wedding can be extremely helpful to engaged couples who are working out the details of their own ceremony. If you are planning a wedding, look around in your area for interfaith couples who would be willing to share their experiences with you. You may even live in an area where an established interfaith group exists, and you can draw on the experiences and insights of a whole roomful of interfaith families. Such groups exist in Chicago, Washington, DC, New Haven, Minneapolis, San Francisco, and other metropolitan areas around the country.

Who better to ask about planning an interfaith wedding ceremony than couples who have already done it? In response to a survey in the February/March 1995 issue of *Dovetail*, readers shared their reflections on their own wedding days. Several common threads emerged. Couples who created their own blended ceremonies were almost universally pleased with the results, and often cited their interfaith ceremonies as "the best part" of their wedding days. On the other hand, couples whose ceremonies included a predominance of traditions from a single faith were often wistful about the lack of balance.

Almost everyone who responded to the survey was pleased with the positive responses of their families on their wedding day, even when families had been distant or disapproving beforehand. A Jewish respondent from Massachusetts, when asked about what she would do differently, reflected on the civil ceremony performed by a Jewish judge, and said that she would have "involved more people, like our parents, in the ceremony. At the time, they did not appear to wish to be involved."

A New York respondent who has been married for 18 years remembers that the best part of her wedding day was "the ceremony, which we had written ourselves." The ceremony was officiated by a New Jersey rabbi, and the families, who had initially expressed concerns about the difficulties of raising interfaith children, were present and supportive on the wedding day.

Likewise, the best part of one Pennsylvania couple's wedding was "our interfaith ceremony. We spent a lot of time working on the details because this was very important to both of us. We were thrilled with the result." They had expected their families "to be polite and respect our interfaith ceremony. We were surprised and delighted to see everyone from both families having such a good time and really enjoying each other's traditions."

A Texas couple remembers the highlight of its church wedding as "having both faiths strongly represented in one blended ceremony." This couple worked hard at "building our own special service," which included a minister from the church of the bride's family and a rabbi from the groom's childhood synagogue. The bride has since converted to Judaism, and she wishes she had chosen "a more neutral location, not in the church like we did."

Perhaps the most important lesson that couples can take from these experiences is that great care should be taken in the planning of the wedding ceremony itself. Rather than allowing extended family to guide the process, couples should work out between the themselves what they want to say with their ceremony. They should choose officiants carefully. They should work together to select readings and rituals that are meaningful to both of them. Interfaith partners who work together to discuss their values and identify what is meaningful to each of them in the wedding ritual will do much more than plan their wedding day. They will have a head start on the challenges and opportunities that will face them throughout their spiritual life together.

CHAPTER FOUR

How Can You Celebrate in Your Interfaith Home?

One of the biggest challenges facing a newly established interfaith family is the creation of a home that feels comfortable and meaningful to both partners. Interfaith families cannot rely instinctively on their childhood religious traditions to provide a year-round framework for their homelife. Not every tradition or ritual with which either partner grew up will fit into their emerging interfaith home. Many closely held rituals—from the decoration of a Christmas tree (see Chapter Five for the special issues that arise at holiday time) to the hanging of a mezuzah on the door—have to be explored and negotiated.

Interfaith couples can choose several general routes. They can attempt to incorporate all of the meaningful traditions each partner has experienced, creating a very full and busy household. They can choose to focus on the traditions and rituals of one partner's faith, giving their household a specific religious identity. Or they can choose to allow their home to evolve, remaining flexible in their decisions and trying new things each season or year, sticking with those that work and letting go of those that don't, until over time they have developed a unique family pattern of celebration. Unfortunately, many families simply avoid the choice, allowing their homelife to be largely empty of meaningful ritual, shaped by piecemeal decisions made without careful reflection.

Adina Davidson and Joel Nitzberg, partners in an interfaith marriage, raising two school-age children, facilitate groups for interfaith and intercultural couples in the Boston area. "Many of us when we intermarry are not fully in touch with the potential losses or dilemmas we will face in the future. We may be unformed in our faith identity or we might just be emotionally unprepared. Often, it is when we are actually faced with 'otherness' in our own home that we realize what most connects us to our own traditions."

Here are a few suggestions from Davidson and Nitzberg that might help as you begin to establish your common home:
- Be honest. Push yourself to say what is true for you. Fear is often the biggest inhibitor of straight talk, but holding back makes it impossible for real needs to get met and keeps the relationship fragile rather than allowing it to strengthen.
- Let go. Face the reality that you or your partner may never truly "understand" each other's position. Ironically, connection may be more possible when couples stop expecting to change one another's point of view.
- Empathize, empathize, empathize. You may not be able to agree with your partner, but you can still feel for him or her. Being empathic is at the core of a couple's ability to weather the storm of interfaith differences and

other differences as well.

- Expect conflict. Disagreements, anger and hurt are all part of the normal resolution of these issues. How to fight while not blaming or being vindictive is something that all couples need to learn.

- Honor the losses. Don't gloss over loss, or put it behind you prematurely. For couples to feel positive about their future, they need to be able to tolerate sadness related to interfaith compromises, without having to "fix it."

- Think and act outside of the box. Experiment. The important issues will keep emerging, giving you many opportunities to experiment and practice different ways of structuring a household. By actively trying different things you will figure out what you can live with and what can be built. Moving forward, however clumsily, will allow you to bump up against what feels right and what doesn't. You can take current holidays and look at how to reshape them based on the needs and associations of both of you. Imagine ways to alter some of the tangible aspects of each of your traditions, as long as you don't lose the essence of the feelings they evoke.

Davidson and Nitzberg tell couples to expect that "this is a lifelong process and time is a very important teacher. The issues will keep surfacing differently as we grow up. It's predictable that some of our choices will remain unresolved for now. Eventually our triggers will become more familiar and we will develop 'equipment' and history that will help give us perspective. Learning to live with what's real and to be forgiving of ourselves will enrich us and make for loving and strong partnerships."

It is for the reason cited above by Davidson and Nitzberg—that our home life is where the deepest and most visceral questions and contradictions between a Jew and a Christian will surface—that it is vital that interfaith couples take time to discuss how they envision their common home. Especially if the couple plans to have children, the establishment of routines and rituals that both partners can enjoy will make their home a stronger place. Discussion of these rituals, while perhaps starting with the obvious—Hanukkah and Christmas, Passover and Easter, the High Holidays, the Sabbath—should eventually deepen to encompass other seasonal, weekly, and even daily traditions.

Rituals help families make sense of their lives. The symbols they use—a prayer, a song, a special food—enable them to find meaning or mark important transitions. For interfaith families especially, the consistent and repeated use of home rituals can help weave a solid and unique family fabric, full of color and texture.

Interfaith families can't help but create rituals. Frequently, sometimes unwittingly, Jewish/Christian couples develop ceremonies and day-to-day rituals that fit their special family situation, using as a foundation their two sets of traditions, heritages and memories. When families are conscious about their ritual-making, they can deepen relationships and forge lasting linkages for generations to come.

When creating family rituals, it is especially important to be clear and open about what the family is doing. Both children and extended families will benefit greatly from discussions of the reasons behind choosing to have a special Friday night dinner or deciding to celebrate Christmas and Hanukkah separately.

Many families find that the development of meaningful rituals is easier when they have written examples to consider (see the Appendix for a list of useful books of prayers to use as a starting point). It is often helpful for interfaith couples who are just starting out to locate and converse with more established interfaith families in their area, in order to get an idea of the variety of challenges and solutions that they may face. A young couple can ask an established couple what it feels like to have a Christmas tree, or to consistently celebrate Shabbat, or to share holidays with both sets of extended family.

Some partners in interfaith families spend a great deal of time and energy developing rituals for their homelife. Laya Tamar, a licensed clinical social worker and a certified Life-Cycle Counselor and Guide in Boulder, Colorado, has worked consciously for years to develop a consistent identity for her interfaith home. The Jewish partner in her interfaith marriage, Tamar is married to a non-practicing Christian. As Tamar prepared for the birth of her first child, she returned to her Jewish roots, and over time Judaism became the family's religious foundation. "I understand now the importance of being an active participant in the creation and implementation of family rituals," she reflects. "Especially for an interfaith couple, a ceremony will truly serve both partners only when it is inclusive of their individual as well as their common needs."

Tamar suggests the inclusion of extended family and friends in an interfaith family's rituals and celebrations. She notes that mealtime, bedtime, and sabbath celebrations are all times that can be imbued with significance, by recognizing their importance as transition times, and by expressing out loud a family's gratitude, prayers, or blessings. "Regardless of our religious background, we can all appreciate the opportunity afforded by observing Shabbat to be more luxurious with our time, to be quiet and reflect, to take a leisurely walk and appreciate what surrounds us." While Tamar's family has chosen to celebrate the Jewish Sabbath, this advice can apply as well to families who choose to honor the Christian Sabbath, or to those who create their own weekly reflection time.

Another veteran to the challenges of establishing a coherent interfaith homelife, Nancy Nutting Cohen is Pastoral Associate at St. Henry's Church in Monticello, Minnesota. She reflects on the unexpected blessings that have come from the conscious development of her interfaith marriage. "We started home celebrations because we felt a need to ritualize important moments in our life and, because of our interfaith status, we didn't feel welcome and/or comfortable approaching our local church or temple," remembers Cohen. "Even after we felt more welcome and comfortable, however, we continued these home celebrations because it felt so right for home to be our place of worship and for us to be the creators and leaders of these rituals."

Following is a sampling of the Cohen family's home rituals:

- Besides the Friday Shabbat service and all of the holiday celebrations that revolve around meals, we include a ritual for every meal. The children take turns choosing the prayer (we have five in our repertoire, mostly generic camp-style songs, but also one Hebrew blessing). Most often, they choose "Johnny Appleseed"—"Oh, the Lord's been good to me, and so I thank the Lord, for giving me the things I need, the sun and the rain and the apple seed. The Lord's been good to me!" And we follow this by everyone sharing how the Lord was good to him/her that day.

- We use a particularly popular meal (a lox and bagel breakfast) to mark birthdays, religious and secular holidays (Mother's Day, Father's Day, Memorial Day, Labor Day, Valentine's Day), and the beginning/ending of school and vacations. Because we like lox and bagels so much, we find lots of things to celebrate!

- One of my favorite blessing rituals is one that my children do to themselves each morning before leaving for school. We have a mirror by the front door, and on their way out, they pause, look at their own reflection surrounded by the rest of us, and say, "Katie, the thing I like most about you is . . ." On those occasional days when they have trouble thinking of something, the rest of us chime in. I especially like that the kids are learning to affirm themselves.

- We use bedtime to reflect and share with our children and each other about when during the day we felt closest to God/people/nature and when we felt most distant.

- Moving into a new house or renovating a portion of the house lends itself well to doing a ritual blessing or dedication. We have gathered friends together and asked them to share their thoughts about what makes a house a home or to state their wish for what good might happen within the walls of that room or house. An art piece, wall hanging, or mezuzah can then be dedicated as a visual reminder of the ritual that has taken place.

- When a couple first learns that they're expecting a baby, they can gather family or friends together to pray a blessing for a healthy pregnancy, a safe delivery, and wisdom and love for the parents.

- Blessing seeds, gardens, and house plants can also be an occasion to reflect on the ways we have grown since we last planted and how we want to grow in the coming season.

- We have a quick and simple ritual for every trip that we take. As we pull out of the driveway, whoever is thinking fastest says, "God, keep us safe on this trip," and everyone else answers, "Amen!" (It started as something I would say, but now the children are beating me to it!)
- For our tenth anniversary, my husband and I decided to renew our marriage vows. We invited the priest-friend who witnessed our wedding to come for dinner, we looked through photo albums, told our kids about our wedding day (for the umpteenth time!), and recited some of the prayers and the vows from our wedding. As a symbol of caring for one another, we (including our children and Father Greg) washed each other's feet, with James Taylor's "Shower the People (You Love With Love)" playing in the background. We had purchased an Israeli sculpture of a four-person family which we blessed, and I put together a framed collection of favorite photos from "The First Ten Years" which we hung on the wall. Finally, after the kids went to bed, Harry and I shared our "pre-arranged but surprise tributes" with each other and Father Greg. I wrote about (and read aloud) the ten things I have come to love most about Harry and he recorded together the portions of love songs that remind him of me. The whole evening was a powerful ritual!
- As part of birthday celebrations, we retell the story of the birth and go through old photos.
- During the High Holidays, we've established the tradition of writing on a page what "I'm proud of . . ." and what "I'll do better at . . ." and then stapling it to the previous year's pages which are bound by decorated construction paper called our "Book of Life." (We've noticed that we tend to be proud of and resolve to do better at pretty much the same things every year. Such is life!)

In creating family rituals, Cohen invites interfaith couples to think about the following:
1) What values are you trying to express? Possibilities include family, growth, forgiveness, awareness of a Higher Power, love, wholeness, etc.
2) What songs, prayers, and readings express those values? Feel free to use contemporary songs and readings (especially children's books!).
3) What action could be used as part of the ritual? You might want to try sharing a meal, giving a hug, writing something, washing feet, lighting a candle, creating something, etc.
4) What symbol can be part of the ritual and then serve as a reminder afterwards? You might use a photo, wall hanging, statue, book, candle, the created something, etc.
5) What key people do you want present and how can they be involved? I

have found that the more people are involved and share what they believe, the more powerful the experience is.

Ideas for Starting Your Own Rituals

- Plan a yearly family get-together. Draw a family tree so that people see how they are connected. Try to locate and invite lost relatives.
- Make your family's holiday meals into potluck affairs to which each guest always brings his or her specialty.
- Incorporate volunteer work into holiday celebrations. Serve Christmas dinner at the local homeless shelter, or help deliver kosher food to the home-bound during Passover. Better yet, schedule a monthly or weekly family service day, when you work together for someone else.
- Pick a day for an annual celebration of your two family's origins, lores and legacies.
- Once a week, have everyone bring something to the dinner table that has special meaning to him or her. Or have each family member bring coins to the Shabbat table each week, in the Jewish tradition of *tzedakah* (Hebrew for 'charity' or 'mutual responsibility'). Collect them in a special container, and when it is full, decide together how the money will be used.
- Build on the anticipation of annual holidays by preparing beforehand. You might share a family Advent calendar before Christmas or a daily activity during the Lenten season.
- Use special candlesticks, tablecloths, flowers, or plates to mark family events. Some families like to have different objects to represent different traditions—a candelabra used only for Jewish holidays, a platter saved especially for the Christmas turkey. Others link their family's cycle of events by using something over and over throughout the year. A simple ceramic pitcher can be used as a vase on *Shabbat*, a vessel for pouring water at a welcoming ceremony, a decanter during the holidays, and the hiding place for small birthday gifts.
- At the beginning of the year, sit down together and create a calendar of the year's special events. Talk about everyday rituals and holiday celebrations. Evaluate the previous year's events, and give each family member time to offer suggestions for changes and additions to the family's ritual life.

How Can Interfaith Families Worship Together?

Another important aspect of setting up an interfaith home is the conscious decision about how and where to worship. Whether as incorporated into a wedding ceremony or as part of a weekly routine, worship is important for the spiritual life and well-being of Jewish/Christian families. Whenever we lift up God's name together we are involved in worship. When we say grace at dinner, when we share a Shabbat dinner or Passover seder with friends, when we create our weddings, baby naming ceremonies, and coming-of-age rituals, we are taking part in worship. When we accompany our spouse to services at his or her religious institutions, we are taking part in worship. When we attend a community-wide Thanksgiving service or listen to a benediction at commencement exercises, we are taking part in worship.

What sets Jewish/Christian families apart, of course, is the interfaith aspect of our families and the different and often conflicting religious traditions with which we must deal in our worship experiences together. This section is an introduction to some of the philosophical, theological and practical issues raised by the topic of interfaith worship.

The National Council of Churches of Christ in the U.S.A. (NCC) Office of Interfaith Relations offers advice to anyone planning or taking part in an interfaith worship experience. "Carefully planned and caringly led, interfaith worship can offer us the opportunity to learn more about each other's religious traditions and expressions, as well as our own, in a context of respect, discovery, and appreciation for the uniqueness and diversity given to us. Interreligious worship is not an attempt to create a new religion by melting down of all those gathered into a neutral worship form. Instead it is a gathering of diverse and unique religious expressions which come together for a common purpose. We come together to celebrate, but each of us brings our own rituals, stories, and acts to help create the worship experience."

Even outside of interfaith families, Jews and Christians do worship together on special occasions. For example, joint Thanksgiving services are quite common. Increasingly, special events such as a memorial to Holocaust victims or prayerful yearnings for peace are commemorated with joint worship.

According to the NCC, "Interfaith worship of this kind signals a new day. Since the human inclination is to stay within our own separate comfortable groups, it can be assumed that those who come to worship in an interfaith setting will be those who choose to break barriers of isolation, antagonism, and mutual suspicion."

Planning Joint Worship

The NCC and the UAHC (the Union of American Hebrew Congregations, the governing body of Reform Judaism) have agreed on common guiding principles for planning interfaith worship, principles which can be incorporated readily into any worship planned by an interfaith family as well. "Two planning principles cannot be overemphasized: (1) that all prayers, readings, homilies—every aspect of the service—should use language which is inclusive of both religious traditions; and (2) that the emphasis should be on that which points us to our common heritage in God and to our mutual desire for peace and a just society."

Other principles suggested include: setting the worship service in the sacred space of a synagogue or church, or in an auditorium or other setting with a symbol of each faith present; making a strong effort to assure all who enter that they are most welcome, including deliberate seating together of people from various faith communities, and promotion of conversation before worship; prayers to God alone and not in the name of Jesus or of the Trinity; use of Jewish and Christian scripture, with the aims to select the universal and to emphasize that which unites.[1]

Interfaith Liturgy

The principles listed above are helpful guides as an interfaith family begins to think about how to worship. There are, however, additional questions that must be faced when two faiths coexist—and worship—in one home. One Jewish partner in an interfaith family who has dedicated considerable energy to these questions is Oscar A. Rosenbloom, a member of *Dovetail*'s Editorial Advisory Board, and attorney at Apple Computer. Since 1989 Rosenbloom has been actively involved in the Interfaith Community of Palo Alto, California, for which he has written services and performed as cantor. In this section, he explores the possibility of interfaith groups' developing a liturgy for their worship and provides observations which may be of help to other groups undertaking such an effort.

"When interfaith couples meet together on an ongoing basis and seek to form a community, we must move beyond the religiosity of a single service to the question of whether and how an interfaith liturgy can be created.

"Unlike the early Christian communities who evolved liturgy from their Jewish experience and were motivated to do so out of religious conviction, current day interfaith groups are not formed by people who have banded together out of a conscious conviction of a commitment to shared faith. It is rather the opposite—these groups are created by people who find the absence of a common religious conviction motivates them to seek a group where they can find community in a sense that they do not find as a couple within their faith communities of origin.

"My sense is that such interfaith communities will have limited success in creating an interfaith liturgy. The more realistic expectation for such groups is to create interfaith services for life-cycle events and provide a nurturing environment in which to educate the members about each other's faith traditions.

"The central difficulty in developing any interfaith liturgy has to do with the divinity of Jesus. While the person of Jesus can be interesting to Jewish spouses, the divinizing of Jesus in liturgy becomes a fact of such discomfort that it prevents a liturgy from evolving within these groups. To develop a liturgy with any Christological component would be tantamount to making the liturgy Christian. To omit the divinity of Jesus is tantamount to making the liturgy Jewish.

"In the nine years of the Interfaith Community of Palo Alto, most services have celebrated Jewish holidays while giving explanations of the links in the service to the experience of Jesus as a Jew and/or recognizing Jesus as a teacher within the context of the service.

"For example, at Passover, we have a seder celebration in which we incorporate reference material explaining the biblical commandment to celebrate the Passover, and point out the relationships of that commandment to the Last Supper. There has been a reading within the service which is clearly Christian in tone, yet without reference to Jesus. At the Christmas/Hanukkah season, it is more possible to have a celebration in which the symbol of light in the Hanukkah candle and the advent candle can be combined.

"The most difficult time to reach any accommodation with this central difficulty is the celebration of Easter. It is here that there is no shared symbolism and no possibility of authentic religious observance without divinizing Jesus.

"My experience with this limitation has been that while an interfaith group can have meaningful worship experiences, introduction of the divinity of Jesus acts as a severe restraint on any such experience. That has occurred also in the context of the interfaith marriages at which I have co-officiated.

"Interfaith groups do have a significant role to play, and communities of some sort can exist within such groups. I think, however, that those who expect such groups to develop an interfaith liturgy will be disappointed."

Music in Interfaith Worship

It is difficult to imagine a worship service that does not include some type of music. Per Harling, a composer and World Council of Churches consultant on worship, writes that "Music is an international language. Through it we may sense each other's cultures and even come to understand something of the circumstances in which different music is created . . . . There is power in music. Songs may not change the world, but they will never cease to be instruments of hope in hopeless situations, of power in powerless lives, of praise to the incarnated God."

One shining example of the way music can be used to bring people of different faiths together in worship is the April 7, 1994, Papal Concert to Commemorate the Holocaust, hosted by Pope John Paul II in the Vatican. This concert, performed by the Royal Philharmonic Orchestra and the 500-year-old Vatican Capella Giulia Choir, was marked by the first ever visit of a rabbi to the Vatican to co-officiate at a public function. It was also the first time the Vatican had commemorated the Holocaust and the first time Jews and Catholics had prayed together, each in their own way, under the Vatican's roof. After this concert, the Pope spoke: "The melodies and songs that re-echoed in this auditorium were the expression of a common meditation and a shared prayer. Different voices blended in a unison of sounds and harmonies which moved and involved us intimately."

The great tradition of folk songs in support of peace, justice and fellowship can be an asset to any interfaith service. **Shiron L'Shalom**[2], edited by Ann Carol Abrams and Lucy Joan Sollogub, is one collection of such songs with notation for voice and guitar. It includes helpful comments on the origin of each of the selections. Of particular interest will be "Sim Shalom/Dona Nobis Pacem" which provides Hebrew and Latin text to Palestrina's Latin round and creates a lovely bridge between Catholic and Jewish traditions. The inclusion of the spiritual "Down By The Riverside" provides a good reminder of the riches available in the spiritual and gospel traditions.

Another source is the music of the hymns. While musical traditions may be different, texts, particularly those drawn from the Psalms, will be shared. One interesting exception to this rule is the Protestant hymn "The God of Abraham Praise," which is based upon the well-known Jewish doxology, Yigdal. The Methodist preacher Thomas Olivers heard the Yigdal sung in the Great Synagogue in London and, being taken with the music, adopted it in 1772 to Christian lyrics. The current text has been rewritten in universal language which is acceptable to both Jews and Christians and is particularly appropriate for use in interfaith services.

Worship Etiquette

Often people feel ashamed when they go to a church, synagogue, mosque, or other place of worship whose customs are not familiar. You want your spouse to attend Midnight Mass at Christmas, or a bar mitzvah comes up in your family and you want your spouse to come along. Here are some suggestions to make it a little easier.
1. Tell your spouse what to expect. Go through the order of worship before you go. Advise him or her about appropriate attire.
2. Get a book or pamphlet from your church or temple that explains a little about their worship services.
3. Let your spouse know that they can just sit through the service and observe. They are not required to participate.
4. Try to sit in a place that is not too conspicuous. Sitting to the side or

50

toward the back may help your spouse feel more comfortable.

5. Before you go, explain what this ritual means to you and why it is important for you to attend.

6. Go with friends or family. This may make it easier for you and your spouse to feel supported.

7. If there are parts of the service that only members can participate in (for example, receiving communion in the Catholic church), be sure to explain that beforehand.

8. Quietly explain what's happening or what is going to happen next during the service so that your spouse won't always be the last to stand, kneel, etc.

9. Assure your spouse that the important thing is that he/she was considerate enough to come with you because he/she knew it was important to you and you appreciate that sign of love.

Humor in an Interfaith Home

It is easy for interfaith couples and their extended families to take the issues facing them, like the issue of how to worship together, with great seriousness. After all, this is a difficult and challenging path we are choosing, and we must prepare ourselves with the utmost reflection and concentration for what we are doing. But every once in a while—in fact, quite frequently—it is appropriate to allow ourselves to laugh at the situations we encounter. For all families, but especially for interfaith families, laughter is a great tension reliever, a wonderful stress reducer, and a way to open ourselves to the joy and wonder of what is unfolding in our lives.

Below is the story of how one interfaith family makes conscious use of humor in their daily life. Brad Bickford, a clinical social worker in Washington, DC, and the Jewish partner in an interfaith marriage, often uses "laughter therapy" in his work and at home.

"My wife and I are both clinical social workers. Our work is very demanding and stressful. We have a busy household, with a pre-teen and a nine-year-old who acts like a union organizer and socialite. We also have a cockapoo dog who pulls used tissues out of our trashcans and needs to be walked at night when it's ten degrees and snowing.

"My wife and I are part of the sandwich generation, caring not only for our children but also for our aging parents. We use humor to get us through all of this. We try to laugh as much and often as we can.

"A good laugh produces the natural tranquilizers called endorphins. In addition, a good laugh is like a good aerobic workout. Our blood pressure goes up, our heart beats quicker, our breathing accelerates, the muscles in our face and abdomen tighten, our skin tingles and our eyes may water. People with a sense of mirth can cope better with various stresses whether they are infectious, work-related, or other.

"Here are ten of our favorite fun and humorous ways to enjoy life:

1. Laugh spontaneously with your kids for ten seconds or more (five if you have a teenager ... or you can cry—just kidding). Just start laughing and continue it.
2. Tickle your kids or spouse or friend for at least ten seconds.
3. Be sure to take advantage of certain holidays like Halloween and wear a costume to work or at night.
4. Watch comedies on TV or video.
5. Read the cartoons in the Sunday paper and buy cartoon books.
6. Share some humorous experience.
7. Look for the humorous lining in all serious or stressful situations and experiences (it's OK to do so!).
8. Get out and play with your kids. Do what they like to do.
9. Imitate your kids periodically when they act weird or crazy.
10. Make faces with or at your kids or significant other to see who can make the other laugh first."

Says Bickford: "We've learned to cope with life by laughing more, and our interfaith family is a happy one. We hope your family is, too."

CHAPTER FIVE

How Do You Handle the Holidays?

Holidays tend to be one of the most stressful times for interfaith families. Along with life-cycle events such as weddings, baby namings, and coming-of-age ceremonies (see Chapter Eight), the holidays are the most emotional and tradition-laden times to be navigated. Both Jewish and Christian partners in interfaith relationships come with specific and deeply held ideas about how each holiday should be done, and how each was done in their families of origin. Often it takes years of experience and negotiation to come to common ground, where both partners feel comfortable with their family holiday style.

One very helpful tactic for interfaith couples to take as they strive to navigate the holiday seasons (the winter holidays of Christmas and Hanukkah, and the spring holidays of Easter and Passover) is to plan time for calm discussion well before, and after, the holiday schedule gets underway. If a couple can sit down in September or October and map out their strategy for the winter holidays, it can avoid the pressure that inevitably comes as the season opens. And if that couple can take time again in January or February to evaluate its satisfaction and enjoyment of the holidays just passed, it can learn which experiences to reinforce and which to eliminate from next year's holiday schedule. The same holds true for the spring holidays.

Facing the December Dilemma

Starting as early as August or September, in the stores and on the streets, the signs of the winter holiday season are prominently displayed. For a family trying to maintain its own delicate balance between two faiths, the onslaught of Christmas (and to a lesser degree, Hanukkah) symbols can feel like a personal attack.

Why are these symbols—the Christmas tree in particular—so difficult for interfaith families to deal with? How can we balance the bombardment of Christmas cheer with our celebration of Hanukkah, a relatively minor Jewish holiday? And how can we move beyond objects with secular roots to commemorate the true significance of these two distinct and wonderful holidays?

Every interfaith family faces its own so-called December dilemmas: whether or not to have a Christmas tree, whether to wrap presents in Hanukkah or Christmas paper, with which extended families to celebrate (and which services, if any, to attend), which holidays to share with children and to what extent. Under all of these December questions runs a tension that threatens to spoil what should be a joyful and renewing time of year.

But there is no reason for despair. With careful thought and commitment, every Jewish/Christian family can find its own unique answers to tough holiday questions. Difficult though it might be, each family can confront the dilemmas and decide together which aspects of their diverse heritages they will lift up and celebrate in December.

It is not easy to make these decisions at holiday time. An interfaith family cannot escape the flood of holiday images in stores and in the media. Strong childhood memories can pull interfaith couples in opposite directions. Christians who grew up with the "warm fuzzies" of Christmas often cannot understand why their Jewish spouse isn't as sentimental as they are. Jews whose upbringings were devoid of Christmas symbols may feel as if they are betraying their heritage by having a decorated evergreen in their homes. Younger couples can often laugh off these tensions, but when children enter the picture, heartfelt issues can no longer be avoided. Children, whose questions may seem simple, often get right to the core of the holiday matter. "Are you Jewish or Christmas?" they ask with childishly innocent directness.

Again, such memories and symbols are unavoidable, but an interfaith family can decide how it will view and interpret them. Jewish/Christian families have a unique opportunity to give and receive, to embrace both cultures, to celebrate the best of both traditions. Both spouses can respect and enjoy the traditions and rituals of the December holidays without relinquishing or undermining their own beliefs or their joint family decisions. Christian families can appreciate the struggle for religious freedom remembered at Hanukkah. Likewise, a family that has decided to raise its children as Jews can appreciate and celebrate Christmas for its universal cultural significance.

We would be naive if we failed to acknowledge the stress felt by all families, interfaith or same-faith, during the hustle and bustle of December. The combination of family get-togethers, gift-giving, special meals, extra religious services, school programs, and office parties is enough to fill to overflowing the calendar of any family. Interfaith families in particular can lessen the holiday pressure by realizing that not all of their December dilemmas come from trying to balance two traditions.

Beneath all the busyness, the questions and tough decisions, there is something magical about the December holidays. People hum carols and smile more than usual. There is a pervasive feeling of forgiveness and charity, and people take great pleasure in giving freely and without hesitation. Special foods and warm family gatherings create good feelings and lifelong memories. Interfaith families can use this time as an opportunity for thoughtful growth, for celebration of time-honored rituals and creation of meaningful new traditions, for drawing parents and children closer together. By accepting with sensitivity and an open mind the challenge to grow, interfaith families can turn their December dilemmas into December discoveries.

Look for the deepest meaning in each holiday, and see how both Christmas and Hanukkah hold a special message for all humanity. Watch for the times when symbols coincide: the light that radiates from both the candles in the menorah and the lights on the Christmas tree, the freedom signified by both the victory of the Maccabees and the birth of Jesus. These are two different holidays, yes, but as interfaith families, we are uniquely blessed with the opportunity to experience and share the vitality of both important messages.

No matter how you decide to celebrate Hanukkah and Christmas with your partner and children, keep these four key elements in mind: fun, food, festive decorations, and family togetherness. Make sure that you include all four of these elements in your celebrations.

Unitarian Universalist minister Forrest Whitman, who has served a large number of Jewish/Christian families in several congregations around the country, offers interfaith families this suggestion: "Share with joy your own religious experience. Tell your children what your personal spiritual experience is like, how you have come to stand in awe before the Holy. If this experience is centered in an historical religious community, let them know that. Our children want to know what the transcendent means in our lives. They want to know where our faith was nurtured even if they one day choose another faith community or none at all."

Becky Seashore, the adult child of an interfaith family, is now active with both a Hillel group and as advisor to an independent interfaith family group in New Haven, Connecticut. She offers the following reflections on her experiences with the winter holidays.

"Because the majority culture in the United States is derived from Christianity, and because Judaism as a minority culture fears assimilation, the temporal coincidence of Hanukkah and Christmas assumes great significance in society, particularly for those of us who are members of interfaith families.

"The use of Hanukkah for celebrating cultural distinctiveness is not bad at all. But the majority culture from which Judaism distinguishes itself is no longer Christianity per say but the religion of 'America,' of which Christmas is an integral part. While the two holidays have different histories, I think Hanukkah and Christmas have much in common, and interfaith families are in the best position to take advantage of their rich associations.

"Although Hanukkah's story of an ancient victory against Hellenization has had an enduring impact on Jewish conciousness and practice, the foremost association of the holiday for most people is not the battlefield but the menorah and God's miracle of the everlasting oil. Christmas is also a holiday that attributes to God the production of a miracle of light—the star that guides the way to the manger in Bethlehem. (It is interesting to note that pagan holidays occurring in winter also utilize the themes of light and hope, and it is from them that symbols such as the Christmas tree—also traditionally decorated with lights—are derived.)

"Similarly, the tradition of gift giving, despite protests of commercialization, is an authentic and integral feature of both stories. For what reason was the Temple in the story of Hanukkah rededicated after the Greek altars were removed if not for the offering of gifts to God? And with what did the wise men approach the baby Jesus but gifts of frankincense and myrrh?

"Finally, while the miraculous ritual oil that God made was of a private nature, burning deep within the Temple, the rabbinic laws relating to Hanukkah maintain that a menorah must be put in a window or other public place. Likewise, the intimacy of the creche stands in contrast to the guiding star which attracted the attention of shepherds and kings alike. To me, this suggests the transformative potential of these holidays: that when a group is secure in its inner space it can be, as another shared Judeo-Christian source (Isaiah) describes, 'a light unto the nations,' promoting a vision of tolerance and peace. Private yet public, intimate yet individual: in pursuing and exemplifying this balance, secure interfaith families can lead the way, letting their own lights shine."

Practical Advice for Navigating the Winter Holidays

Mary Rosenbaum, award-winning co-author of **Celebrating Our Differences: Living Two Faiths in One Marriage**, has been intermarried for over 30 years. She is an active member of St. Patrick Catholic Church in Carlisle, Pennsylvania, where she has been a lector for twenty-five years. Rosenbaum suggests that the difficulty interfaith couples have with the winter holidays often "really has to do with defining what parts of the celebrations are actually religious and which are cultural and nostalgic." She cites four different scenarios for how couples see the winter holidays, and suggests that if a couple takes the time to identify which scenario rings true for them, they will discover another positive aspect to interfaith marriage: "In addition to finding out about someone else's religion, you're likely to spend a lot more time reexamining and learning about your own. With diligence, and a bit of luck, both of you will acquire real appreciation for both faiths." Following are Rosenbaum's four holiday scenarios:

1. Both Jew and Christian are comfortable with a secular celebration. This is an easy one. All you have to do is define what is unacceptably religious to either of you. You probably won't display a creche. You may feel that elaborate outdoor decorations are out of place. If you play seasonal music, you'll stick to "Jingle Bells" and "White Christmas" while leaving "O Holy Night" alone.

2. The Christian wants a religious Christmas, while the Jew sees it as a pleasant nonreligious observance. You'll have to tread a little lightly here.

The Christian will have to remember that the essence of Christmas takes place in the heart, not in the decor or even in church. The Jew should be sensitive to the offensiveness of much modern secularization to the religious Christian and not blithely assume that an electrified Rudolph on the roof says it all.

3. The Christian, or rather gentile, is the secularist, while the Jew is uncomfortable with any sort of celebration. The Christian should keep in mind that even that patron saint of conspicuous consumption, Santa Claus, was originally a medieval bishop and saint, so that electric Rudolph is actually a sort of twice-removed reminder of religious content. The Jew must recognize that practices with their roots in memories of happy family occasions can't be cavalierly dismissed without causing resentment.

4. Both Christian and Jew have strong religious commitments. This, surprisingly, can be easier to deal with than the last two. What you do here is take all the above advice, combine it with a sense of humor and lots of good will, and work out the practical aspects step by step.[1]

When Children Are Part of Your Holidays

Navigating the winter holidays can be challenging when a couple is on its own; when children enter the picture, the path becomes even more frought with challenges. Interfaith parents who have been through the strenuous process of creating meaningful holiday experiences for their families often feel as if they have accomplished a marvelous feat. Such families are eager to share their experiences and ideas, and to lend their support to families just starting out.

A December Compromise

Susan W. Hammond is a child psychologist and a Quaker. She lives with her husband and son in the Washington, DC, area. "When I was a child," she remembers, "my Quaker family usually invited others to our holiday celebrations, believing that it added excitement as well as meaning to the holiday. On Christmas Eve, we often included a couple we knew. He was Jewish and she Episcopalian, and they had agreed when they married to celebrate only the Jewish holidays in their home. The woman always seemed eager to share our Christmas. I remember thinking that it was sad that in order to celebrate what was obviously an important holiday for her, she had to visit with friends.

"I started thinking about this couple again when I was dating my now-husband, who is Jewish. As we gradually became more serious about each other, we began to discuss the question of how to celebrate the holidays of our two religions. At first it was easy: we spent the Jewish holidays with his family and the Christian ones with mine; I gave him Hanukkah presents and he gave me gifts at Christmas. But as we became closer we agreed that it was important to us to establish our own holiday traditions, and to celebrate together.

"As we experimented with ways of observing the holidays, we found three dimensions along which we needed to negotiate a compromise. The first was that each of us needed to feel that our favorite holidays had been properly celebrated. For me, the solution reached by the couple from my childhood seemed like a bad choice for us; I could no more celebrate Christmas only at someone else's home than my husband could just skip Hanukkah. I needed to have a tree in the living room and a wreath on the door; for my husband, lighting the Hanukkah candles every evening was important.

"We also wanted to make the celebration something that we both participated in. We have each found aspects of the holidays that we both enjoy, which allows us to have a family celebration. But this also required compromise, along a second dimension: the celebration in the home needed to be within our level of comfort with the other's religion.

"This was a greater issue for my husband than for me for the December holidays. He initially felt that participating in a Christmas celebration was in some way a betrayal of his own religion. (I have found that Passover brings up more comfort issues for me, with its talk of the uniqueness of the Jewish people.) We started out with a sparsely decorated tree, and over time have added a wreath, hung stockings, and put up other decorations. My husband especially likes the mistletoe. However, we did agree to avoid the most overtly Christian symbols, such as a creche, leaving those for our visits to my parents. For Hanukkah we use a menorah which I gave my husband while we were dating, and light candles and eat traditional foods.

"As we began celebrating both holidays together, we discovered a third issue where compromise was required: avoiding overkill. If we didn't want to spend all of November and December celebrating holidays, as well as blow out the family budget on an indulgent number of gifts, we had to find some way to cut back. So we agreed to limit our gift-giving within the family by alternating between the holidays. One year we give each other Hanukkah presents, and the next year we do more for Christmas. We still receive Hanukkah gifts from his family and Christmas presents from mine, so both holidays include the excitement of opening presents, but the holiday season is now less overwhelming.

"Despite the tensions and compromises, we have both come to enjoy aspects of the other's favorite holidays. In addition, I have found that one great advantage of intermarriage is that there is no competition between our family holiday traditions. If I want to put the tree up on Christmas Eve, no one says, "But in my family we always did it in mid-December." And we have each added to the family traditions for both holidays. My husband has started picking out Christmas tree ornaments and recently convinced me to decorate the tree with clear lights instead of colors, and I have taught him to make decorated cookies in the shapes of menorahs and dreidels.

"I also think that developing these traditions has strengthened our relationship as a couple. The process of finding a satisfactory compromise helped us become more sensitive to the other's perspective and taught us ways of negotiating which we apply in other situations. And celebrating the holidays together, rather than each of us observing a separate occasion, makes us feel like a strong family.

"We now have a son with whom to share our emerging traditions. We are working to find ways to include him in our pleasure in the holidays, without lapsing into doing too much for both holidays. I'm glad we had a few years to become comfortable with our arrangement; by now, this is our own family tradition."

A Different Kind of Holiday Present

Kris Garnjost is a freelance writer and stay-at-home dad. His wife Lori Hirshfield is a community planner for the Arlington County government in northern Virginia. They live with their daughter in Falls Church, Virginia.

"My wife and I met because of what we hold to be the true spirit of the Christmas and Hanukkah holidays—giving the gift of ourselves to others. Actually, if it weren't for this spiritual connection between the holidays, we probably never would have met. Luckily for us, there were a bunch of other people who saw a similar connection, and they formed a volunteer organization called The Holiday Project.

"On Christmas Day and during Hanukkah, The Holiday Project takes the holiday celebration of sharing and hope to people confined to nursing homes, hospitals, and correctional facilities. Thousands of volunteers all over the country take time during their holidays to spend time with people in hundreds of facilities.

"This project flies in the face of the hype and commercialism that has taken over the holidays. I know that at least one day a year I can make a difference in somebody else's life.

"Once we were touched by the special experience of these visits, we wanted to make sure others got to visit too. That's how we met. We were both attending the 1988 Holiday Project National Conference. I was chairman of The Holiday Project chapter in Burlington, Vermont, and Lori was on the chapter steering committee for Washington, D.C.

"Now we are married and live in the Washington, D.C. area with our daughter, Rachael. Since she was five months old, Rachael has been charming nursing home residents on Mother's Day, Father's Day, Veteran's Day, Hanukkah, and Christmas Day.

"Our participation in The Holiday Project has made celebrating the holidays quite easy to resolve. When Lori requested that our children be raised in the Jewish faith, it was relatively simple for me to say yes. I have no strong attachment to Christian traditions. I grew up going to a Unitarian Sunday school that could be described as a study of the world's great religions.

"The one point that could have been difficult was Christmas. Although not a religious occasion for my family, the Christmas celebrations I grew up with do hold a place in my heart. Since it was my job on Christmas morning to give out the presents, I felt like I was part of every gift that was given. I was part of every smile, laugh, or whoop of joy.

"The Holiday Project offers me the opportunity to do this many more times on Christmas morning than I ever had in the past, and much more. Going on the visits and being part of organizing the visits means I get to share that feeling with lots of other people. Now that we have Rachael, I get to offer a gift that's more precious and more appreciated than anything I have ever given or received. It is amazing to see how moods change when she comes into a room.

"We have chosen to only celebrate Hanukkah in our home; we do this by lighting the menorah candles each night and saying the prayers. I don't miss my family Christmas traditions because we have created new traditions of our own around The Holiday Project visits. Lori says it this way: "The holidays are about getting up in the morning on one day of Hanukkah and on Christmas Day and going to a nursing home and sharing ourselves."

"Our gift exchange is minimal, and often is spread out over the whole month of December. Some of it falls during Hanukkah, some around Christmas, and even as late as New Year's Eve. Since Rachael will be old enough to begin to appreciate presents this year, there may be a bit more structure. It still will not be the focus; we want her holidays to be about the menorah candles, the prayers, and giving of herself on a Holiday Project visit during Hanukkah and Christmas.

"Eventually, I'm sure Rachael will ask why we visit people on Christmas Day but don't have a Christmas tree and don't celebrate Christmas. We plan to tell her what Lori was told when she was a child. "It's like celebrating someone else's birthday—you can celebrate it with them, but it's not your birthday." By that time, I predict that Rachael will be as attached to The Holiday Project as we are."[2]

Making Peace with the Christmas Tree

Nancy Nutting Cohen is a member of the editorial advisory board of *Dovetail: A Journal by and for Jewish/Christian Families*. She lives with her family in Minneapolis, Minnesota, and works as a Pastoral Associate at St. Henry's Church in Monticello, Minnesota. She is a Roman Catholic married to a Jewish man.

"Years ago, my husband and I attended a discussion series on issues facing interfaith couples. By the end, four of the six meetings had eventually evolved into a lengthy and heated exchange about the significance of the Christmas tree. Over the years, I've continued to be amazed at how emotionally charged the issue of the Christmas tree is. And I find myself in the midst of a strange contradiction. On the one hand, I have Jewish friends insisting (almost to the point of foaming at the mouth) that the Christmas tree is a Christian symbol. On the other hand, I have my own childhood memories of nuns and priests ranting (again almost foaming at the mouth) about families who miss the point of Christmas because they put up decorated trees instead of Nativity scenes.

"The fact is the Christmas tree originated as a pagan symbol among nature worshippers during the ancient Roman and Teutonic era. When Christianity spread across Europe, the converts were forbidden to decorate evergreens because their use was associated with pagans. It wasn't until the sixteenth century that Christians started using the tree to express their faith that Jesus was the Tree of Life.

"Today and for most people, however, I suspect the Christmas tree represents fond childhood memories rather than faith statements about what Jesus means to them. And that's fine! Fond childhood memories are important to nurture and pass on. But that's not identical to or exclusive of religion or Christianity. I know many intelligent and thoughtful people who consider themselves atheists/agnostics and have for any number of reasons rejected organized religion, but who still put up Christmas trees and would be very insulted to have that interpreted as a religious symbol.

"Over the fifteen years of our interfaith relationship, my own observance of the December dilemma has evolved into three threads that weave together to form what I feel is a beautiful, comforting, and inspirational blanket. This blanket wraps together and warms the whole family during a time of year that would otherwise be cold and bleak.

"One thread is Hanukkah with its inspiring themes of freedom, miracles, and faithfulness to one's values even in the face of opposition. We celebrate that by lighting candles, retelling the story and sharing how it applies today, playing dreidel, eating latkes, having special time with family and friends, and giving gifts.

"Another thread is Christmas, which leads to thoughts of how Christ is present in the world today, what it means to be human, and how we can work for peace and goodwill toward all. We observe this with a manger scene, family gatherings, letters to distant friends, service projects, songs (about mangers and angels, not sleighbells and chestnuts), and yes, gift-giving. People sometimes comment, 'Your kids must get a lot of gifts!' Truthfully, our kids probably get fewer than their friends. We believe in simplicity and put a lot of thought into keeping the gift-giving within pretty strict limits.

"The final thread is all the secular influence which I group together as Winter Solstice observance. Living in Minnesota where the winters are long, dark and cold, I take great consolation in knowing that after December 21, each day sees a little more sun. I have learned to really appreciate the outdoor lighting that many people put up, not just for December, but beginning right after Halloween and extending through March. We brighten the outside darkness (and our spirits) by decorating a tree. Santa makes a visit, filling stockings and leaving a book, but we don't try to draw a connection between him and the Christ-child (although his origins as St. Nicholas make him one of the few truly Christian symbols). We listen to "White Christmas" and attend the parties. In short, we create fond childhood memories for our children. But we don't confuse this with religious observance, except to acknowledge the elements of joy and goodwill common to both.

"Over the years I have had one significant realization as a result of the oft-repeated Christmas tree discussion, and that realization makes me rather sad. We Christians really aren't very clear about our symbols. If Jews are going to be offended by any symbol (and I'm not trying to offend anyone here), it should be the Nativity scene, not the Christmas tree. We Christians aren't clear about what is at the core of our faith. The tree and Santa are wonderful symbols. I wouldn't want to lose them. They evoke feelings of warmth, happy children, family togetherness, beautiful sights, generosity, love and peace. But there's more to the tradition. And that more often gets lost in the excitement over those two symbols. Frankly, I'm tired of having my religious beliefs reduced to and mistaken for that.

"Hopefully the whole Christmas tree discussion between interfaith couples will push both parties to look more deeply into their own faiths. By pinpointing the key issues and values, sharing those with one another, and identifying what they really want to pass on to their children, couples will be able to weave together the many threads that create both a rich spiritual tradition as well as fond childhood memories."

Questions Kids Ask About the Holidays

How can parents in interfaith families prepare for the winter holidays? One obvious way is to think through how to explain Christmas and Hanukkah to the children, and how a family's actions and observations complement these explanations. Following are the questions asked by a number of interfaith families. These questions have been drawn from a number of sources, including a program called "Questions Kids Ask," which was sponsored by the Outreach program of Jewish Family Service in New Orleans, Louisiana, where interfaith parents who had made the decision to raise their children as Jews could share and discuss the difficult questions posed by their children. Here are some of the questions these parents, and others who have made different decisions about raising children, have struggled with on the topic of the December holidays. All of the names have been changed.

Dawn (Christian married to a Jewish man): My preschooler daughter is figuring out "who goes where." She goes through whole lists of people, from the other kids in nursery school to the members of our extended families, asking questions until she figures out that Grandma has Christmas, Aunt Rhonda has Hanukkah, Uncle Mark has Hanukkah, Cousin Josie has Christmas. And Mommy, Daddy, and I get to have both! She asks why everybody doesn't have both Christmas and Hanukkah. I explain that some people are Jewish, and some people are Christian. Since in our family, Mommy is Christian and Daddy is Jewish, we celebrate both Mommy's and Daddy's holidays. So far, that answer has been enough. It helps, I know, that both my husband and I have learned enough about each other's traditions that we can each answer her questions about both holidays. He can tell her about the birth of baby Jesus, and I can describe the bravery of the Maccabees. Someday, I'm sure, she'll decide she likes one holiday more than the other, or she'll push us harder about how we can have both. Then I guess we'll have the more difficult conversations about her religious identity as the child of an interfaith family. But my husband and I are committed to having her learn about and understand both of our holiday traditions. We know that someday she may choose to identify with only one religion, but at least she'll be comfortable with both. And that comfort is really helpful already—she loves lighting the menorah and decorating the tree! And she tells her simple version of the Hanukkah and Christmas stories to all her friends and relatives, Jews and Christians alike.

Julie (convert to Judaism, married to a Jewish man): My daughter gets to have Christmas with my family, but we don't have it in our house. She has always said she wants to have decorations and a tree. The more difficult part is my husband, who is born Jewish, grew up with a Christmas tree, and he said, "Why can't we have a tree?" I said, "Because we're not talking about two Jewish parents." I mean, for born Jews who just choose to have a tree with no religious connection, it's just a pretty ornament, just a decoration. But it's not going to mean that to my daughter. She's not going to be able to differentiate. She's going to say, "I celebrate Christmas," and while my husband doesn't have a problem with that, I do. I hate it when people say I'm not really Jewish. Even my own daughter has said, "You were a Christian." But I converted, and that means that I am Jewish, whether it's by choice or by birth. I am actively seeking anything I can find to connect me to the religion. So I can't have a Christmas tree. This has been a major debate in our family, so last year we got a fake, four-foot white tree. It has white lights and we decorate it with Hanukkah things. My daughter calls it a Hanukkah bush. We've compromised, but it's not necessarily the compromise I wanted to make. I would have liked to keep the holidays totally separate, but again, I back up and I say, well, I don't see Santa as being religious, so I tell my daughter that Santa visits you because Santa visits all good children. Then she says, "Does he visit Melissa?" and I realize, oops! It really is an issue.

Linda (a Jewish woman married to a Catholic man, raising Jewish children): I grew up in a fairly religious family, even though there weren't that many Jews. We would go to our friends' homes to decorate trees, and they would come to our house for holidays. I remember carolling, just because it was fun. Our parents didn't have a problem with it. But my son can't handle Christmas songs. At school last year, they sang a song about Jesus being King, and my son got really upset and told the music teacher, "I'm Jewish and I don't think we should sing this song, because I don't believe that Jesus is King." She sort of blew him off. It's a public school, and they probably really shouldn't sing the song. But he was really upset. I know I used to say, well, it's just a Christmas song (and that's what my daughter would have done), but he's more conscious of being Jewish and different. He might be that way whether or not he had parents of different religions.

My kids have asked things like, "Doesn't Dad feel bad that we don't celebrate Christmas?" or "Shouldn't we be celebrating Christmas for Dad?" I think that came with, "Why can't we celebrate both Christmas and Hanukkah?" We explained that Dad and I decided to raise our kids Jewish, and we didn't want there to be any confusion. We just wanted to celebrate our holidays as a Jewish family, and Dad still celebrates his holidays in his own way. He goes to Mass on Christmas and Easter, since those are his two big holidays, and he feels good about doing it that way.

Dan (a Jewish man married to a Christian woman): Our kids get asked questions about who they are at elementary school all the time, but especially around the holidays. Some kids try to tell them they can be either Jewish or Christian, but they can't be both. But both of our kids have been able to answer their friends with, "In our family, we celebrate both Christmas and Hanukkah. We are respecting and practicing the religions of both of our parents, just like you practice the religion of both your parents at your house." They have also learned to tell their friends about the similarities between the two holidays, things like peace and brotherhood, lighting candles, gift-giving, and remembering the importance of events in history. We're really proud of how comfortable they are with their dual-faith heritage.

Experts suggest that parents take the time to sit down with their children in advance of the holidays, listening to their kids' questions and offering explanations about the traditions their own family will celebrate. Debi Tenner, the mother of two and teacher of the Sunday School class for older children in a New Haven,

Connecticut, independent interfaith group, currently works in the local school system and has been a summer camp educator for the Congregational Churches of Connecticut. Based on her years of experience working with religious education of interfaith children, she offers the following suggestions for what to say to children at holiday-time:

"Talk with your children about whether you are celebrating each holiday on a religious basis or as a cultural/secular holiday (or both). Give them "clues" to look for: lighting Hanukkah, Shabbat, or Advent candles might be signs of the religious meaning of the holidays. Other clues might be reciting prayers, counting blessings, or making a donation to charity. The cultural and secular holiday celebrations clues include decorating, parties, school performances, and gift giving. Older children might study the lunar cycle/calendar or the names of all the months in Hebrew and compare them to the American solar calendar."

Passover and Easter: Two Faiths Celebrate Spring

Sometimes it's a problem, sometimes not. Depending on how the two religious calendars align themselves, Passover and Easter can overlap or be separated by as much as a month. Especially in those years when the first Passover seder happens sometime during Holy Week, Jewish/Christian families are mindful of their common roots and their evident theological differences.

As interfaith families know, where there's a complication, there's room for learning and growth. There are fascinating connections between the two holidays. Some New Testament interpretations of the Last Supper, which Jesus shared with his disciples near the end of his life, portray it as a Passover seder ritual.

In early Christianity, Passover became important for its metaphorical applications. The New Testament is full of Passover symbolism: Christ as the new paschal lamb, sacrificed for the sins of his followers; Christians as the real unleavened bread, in whom the leaven of sin was no longer at work.

As far as we can tell, the earliest followers of Jesus celebrated the Passover in what was then the traditional Jewish way. The celebration of the Resurrection gradually evolved into the celebration of Easter and replaced any celebration of the traditional Jewish Passover. This gradual separation of the two communities, Christian and Jewish, which occurred over the course of centuries, is of pivotal importance.[3]

Christians Celebrate the Passover

A growing number of Christian churches are incorporating aspects of the Passover meal into their worship experiences, mostly by designing Maundy Thursday "model seders" for their congregants. Often Christians try to combine a seder with their own communion service, creating a hybrid that celebrates common elements while minimizing or ignoring the uniqueness of both traditions. Church leaders hope that such "seders" will help Christians gain a better appreciation of Jesus' (and therefore all Christians') Jewish heritage.

But these Christian "seders" are offensive to many in the Jewish community. Many rabbis agree that the Passover seder as it is now observed is significantly different than the seder observed by Jews during Jesus' lifetime. Jewish leaders are concerned that it may be difficult to correct the impression of church members that there are Christian overtones in the seder. Such concern is heightened when church leaders suggest that they are using the seder to enhance their congregants' Easter celebration. The Union of American Hebrew Congregations, the official body of Reform Judaism, states that "it may sometimes be possible to run such a [seder] program successfully, especially when members of the church and synagogue have been involved in a long-term, sustained dialogue and each group is immersed in the history of the other. But that is usually not the case."

Of course, interfaith families celebrate the Passover seder, too, and bring to their celebration Christian perspectives. Hopefully, our different perspectives can heighten, not diminish, the experience.

But What About Easter?

Christians can easily and honestly join their Jewish partners in the celebration of Passover. The seder, as a home ritual, is easy to adapt and expand to incorporate a wider world view. And the central tenet of the seder liturgy—liberation from bondage—is a universally appreciable goal.

It is much more difficult, theologically and culturally, for Jews to join in the celebration of Easter. First, it is a church-based holiday that often seems out of a couple's control. Second, the point of the celebration, the resurrection of Jesus, is unequivocally outside the realm of Jewish belief and tradition. When a Jewish partner agrees to accompany his or her Christian spouse to church on Easter, it is usually with trepidation and guilt. And these feelings are often reinforced in the sanctuary. Many an interfaith couple has a story of a well-intentioned trip to Easter Sunday services, only to be greeted with sermons that blame Jews for Jesus' crucifixion or exclude from salvation anyone who does not believe in the actual physical resurrection of Jesus. Of course, for every such sermon there is also a message by a more liberal, inclusive pastor, who focuses on the potential for rebirth and resurrection in our own lives today. But many Jewish/Christian families have not found a church in which they can hear such an uplifting Easter message. Hopefully, interfaith families who continue to search can find Christian communities which celebrate Holy Week in an open and affirming way.

In a theological sense, the "Spring Thing" far surpasses the December dilemma" in its difficulty of reconciliation. And this is one tension in an interfaith relationship that cannot be fully resolved. Perhaps, as Jewish/Christian couples, having chosen to live together in two separate spheres, we will have to accept that this is one of the times when our beliefs cannot overlap, when we can only accept and celebrate the deep emotions and expectations of our partners for the holidays of their traditions. Perhaps the best we can do is to use the tension we feel as fodder for growth and increased understanding.

Of course, there are ways to make your interfaith family's Easter celebration a positive one. Talk at home about your beliefs and questions. Focus on the universal theme of spring's new growth, and reflect on the possibilities for renewal in your own lives. Enjoy the Easter egg hunts and the fancy clothes, and share special traditions and recipes from your childhood. You may want to distinguish between traditions that are connected theologically to the holiday, such as Easter vigils, and those that have been attached by the secular world, like egg hunts and bunnies. This time of year as always, what Jewish/Christian families do in their homes, how they share ideas and create traditions, is the solid foundation on which two faiths can dovetail.

CHAPTER SIX

How Do You Raise the Children?

Undoubtedly the toughest issue facing interfaith families is knowing whether and how to share two sets of religious beliefs and traditions with children. Intermarried couples on their own can usually resolve religious and cultural differences and find a comfortable common path. When children enter the picture, a whole new set of challenging decisions emerges.

Often the decision to have children upsets what has been a comfortable balance in a two-person interfaith family. Until an interfaith couple has children, the different backgrounds of each partner seem complementary and coexist relatively easily in a home. When children enter that home, however, parents may have to renegotiate, rethinking their commitments to God, to their individual faiths, to their extended families, and to the decisions they've already made. Intermarried couples have to do serious negotiation to come up with a family plan that both meets the needs of each parent and provides for the emotional and spiritual well-being of the children. Often this attention to family spiritual life is a lifelong process, with room for adjustment and revision along the way. And occasionally, when a family's composition changes, whether through death (see Chapter Seven) or divorce (see Chapter Eight), the plan for children's religious education may need to be reviewed and reconsidered.

Whatever a family's ultimate decision, the process of distilling and respecting two sets of spiritual beliefs is a vitally important one. Considering God— whatever that means to you and your spouse—is an important part of being a family. Churches and temples can provide an excellent framework from which to build spiritual beliefs, but these tenets will take hold only when parents make them personal and relevant to everyday life.

And, even if you haven't come up with a plan for your children's religious education, you can't avoid the issue for long. No matter what parents choose to teach or not teach their children, religious symbols and language are so widely present in this society that virtually no child reaches school age without having formulated—with or without religious instruction—their own images of God.

Raising interfaith kids can be a daunting yet exhilarating process. Successful interfaith parents serve as guides for their children's spiritual journeys, relying on a sense of humor, the knowledge that God is there as the ultimate guide, and the ability to trust that things will work out. Interfaith parents should pay attention to their own spiritual lives, heeding the advice of Polly Berrien Berends, author of **Gently Lead, or How to Teach Your Children About God While Finding Out for Yourself**.

In this insightful book, Berends offers a new way of thinking about religious upbringing that is especially pertinent to interfaith families. "Looking at your own tradition by the light of others' is very illuminating. Mostly what we strongly disagree about is what we are both wrong about. Instead of defending our answers we should be deepening our questions." Berend goes on to apply this idea to religious education for young people. "Traditions are wonderful and important, but to impose beliefs is not helpful. I have seen many adolescents lose their faith when they turned for help and found their childhood beliefs meaningless. So it is much better to help young people with their questions than to try to get them to commit to your answers. . . . They [will be] very surprised and relieved to discover that many of the things they have been taught in religious education actually mean something that can be understood and that has to do with their real daily lives. They love to find these ideas presented in the language of other cultures, literature, and religions."

A mother echoed Berends' advice when she told Anthony Brandt, a contributing editor of **Parenting** Magazine: "I think you can transmit values to your kids, but belief is different. Values—respect for other people, respect for life, not taking what doesn't belong to you, things like that—they're universal, they're everywhere. But belief is a special thing. You have to come to it on your own; nobody can impose it on you."

Making a Decision About Religious Identity

Nancy Nutting Cohen, who has been intermarried since 1981 and is raising two adolescent daughters with her Jewish husband Harry, has combined her professional background as a youth minister and religious educator with the practical lived experience of being an interfaith parent searching for answers about religious education.

"Harry and I have chosen to raise our children somewhere between 'one religion with exposure to the other' and 'both religions equally.' We often say we're trying to pass on the best (that is, what's meaningful to us) of both traditions, but I'm not sure how one ever does that equally. We belong to a church and a temple, and take from each what we like and leave the rest. But even more, we do a lot in our home and look to our interfaith couples support group to be a faith community as well. We continually struggle to identify what it is that we believe (not just what our religions have taught us), to share that with one another and the children, and to create rituals in our home that express these beliefs with integrity and a respect for differences. It's been that struggle to identify, share, and express ritually that's been so stretching yet exciting."

Cohen offers a list of key questions an interfaith couple might need to consider:

1) Can you live with the notion that you will never share your religious

beliefs and traditions with your child? Picture what that will look like.

2) If your spouse agrees to raise the children in your tradition and then later finds that s/he can't live with that decision, are you willing and able to renegotiate that decision? In other words, how important is this to you?

3) How knowledgeable and committed are you to your religion, and how much will you need your church or temple's help in providing religious education for your children? Can you do it yourself?

4) How will this decision impact your relationship with your extended family and in-laws?

5) Is your decision fair to yourself? Your spouse? Your children?

Cohen admits that she and her husband have made mistakes and experienced setbacks along the way. She also recognizes the learning and growth that they have enjoyed. She shares some of the perspectives she has gathered over the years:

• Our children are really, first of all, God's children. They don't belong to us or any religion. Our job is to support them on their journey toward God, wherever that might take them.

• Religions (and their doctrines, rituals, and rules) are supposed to point a way to God. No one religion is the only way, nor is the religion supposed to become the god we worship (it's so easy to make that mistake!).

• At least one of the issues in the whole interfaith dilemma is NOT whether individuals are being faithful to their religions, but whether religions are being faithful to their task of supporting people on their journey to God.

• Diversity has become the name of the game of life. The days of Ozzie and Harriet, of neatly defined and predictable family life, are over (if they ever were!). Our children's world will be one where diversity is the norm, rather than the exception. Religion, and the way it is lived out, will be diverse as well.

• Just because we find something new and confusing (like a Jewish/Christian family) doesn't mean our children will find it confusing. They will have ways of making sense of it even if we don't.

• It's as important, if not more, to share our faith (what we believe, what adds meaning to our life) as what our religion teaches.

• All marriages are interfaith marriages. Even when people practice the same religion, they have different images of God, experiences from their own background, levels of intensity, and ideas about how that religion should be lived out.

• We don't have to (and in fact, can't) have all the answers to potential problems beforehand. The important thing is to embark on the journey equipped with good communications skills, mutual respect, creativity and

71

flexibility, and a commitment to keep growing and struggling with the issues.

- A good support system is essential. No matter what course you choose, there will be people who don't understand and who criticize or reject.
- You don't need to worry about "setting an agenda." Children and life experiences will let you know what the next issue is.
- Raising children in a certain religion doesn't guarantee that they'll embrace that religion. All people come to a point in their lives where they must make a choice, that is, find a place that is their spiritual home.

Harmony: The Crucial Factor

David Heller, Ph.D., author of **Talking to Your Child About God: A Book for Families of All Faiths**, offers what he believes to be the most crucial element in interfaith parenting. "You and your spouse must believe in your compatibility and in your harmony with God. And you should convey these ideas to your child. There is nothing more reassuring for an interfaith child than a solid and meaningful parental relationship." In other words, no matter what your plan for religious education, your success depends on how much you believe in, and follow through on, what you're doing.

In **The Intermarriage Handbook**, Judy Petsonk and Jim Remsen list four steps toward untangling the many religious issues faced by an interfaith family: "to figure out your own beliefs and needs, to understand your partner's beliefs and needs, to understand what religious options are available to you as individuals and as a family, and to find a respectful common ground."

The authors assert their finding that "Whether you raise your child in one religion, two religions or no religion has little or no impact on her mental health. But a crucial factor must be present: Both parents must agree with and stand behind the religious pattern you have chosen for your home. In other words, the vital factor in whether your children are happy or unhappy, troubled or secure, is whether the two of you are in harmony."

In her chapter on interfaith marriages, Annette Hollander, author of **How to Help Your Child Have a Spiritual Life: A Parent's Guide to Inner Development** writes: "What parents in mixed marriages can do is create a climate in which the child is not torn between conflicting loyalties, and does not feel that s/he has to choose. Children need to identify with both parents because they love both."

Advice from the Experts

The question of how to raise children in an interfaith family has many answers, and it is the responsibility of each Jewish/Christian couple to sift through the many possibilities in order to find their own personal answer.

Susan Silverman LaDuca, Ph.D., a family therapist in Philadelphia and herself a long-time partner in an interfaith marriage, asserts that "there is no definitive answer to the question regarding religious education for one's children. There is no right or wrong. A couple's decision about provision of formal religious training is a personal one with long-term implications for the children." LaDuca advocates a consensus model, whereby both partners in the interfaith marriage are able to explore and express their views. Her research on interfaith couples found that "the majority of the couples interviewed believed that formal religious training would provide their children with a strong moral and ethical foundation. [However,] the values and ethics that are taught in the family take precedence over those taught elsewhere. The ethics of the home supercede those taught by organized religion."

Interfaith couples, while realizing the validity of LaDuca's observations about the importance of values and ethics being taught in the home, should be aware at the same time of the dangers of syncretism, or combining two religions into a new religious form (see the section on syncretism in Chapter One), which can be confusing at best to young children.

Says Monsignor Edward Connors, retired pastor and Catholic seminary president, who has worked with interfaith couples throughout his career: "Sometimes a couple invents a new religion of their own. They don't realize what they're doing, but they do it. 'On your holy days we'll go there, and on my holy days we'll go here,' and maybe once a month they go to each place apart from the holy days. The impact on the children may not be all that positive. . . . I guess at some point their children will either consider themselves both or will decide that they are one or the other. These families need to find a community of others doing the same thing, so that their children have some context, some community. Many couples who go both ways seem to back into it, with pressure from both families, and are unaware of what they're doing. This choice is filled with difficulties, but I'm not God, I can't say that it might not work for some families. It's certainly better than the other thing that can happen, which is that both partners are considerably weakened in whatever religious practice they have, and they do almost nothing, becoming good humanists."

Rabbi Charles Familant, advisor to the Interfaith Community, an independent group of interfaith families in San Francisco's Bay Area, offers these insights gleaned from years of work with Jewish/Christian families: "Children in interfaith families absorb the state of mind of their parents. If parents are ambivalent or conflicted over their differences, so will be the children. On the other hand, if parents view the home as an opportunity for merging traditional and innovative forms of religious practice and celebration, so will the children.

"Parents have a wonderful opportunity to teach their children, by their par-

ticipation in the many kinds of celebrations, understanding, tolerance, appreciation and love of the other. If the parents promote an atmosphere of honest discussion of their different viewpoints without any attempt to indoctrinate, the children are under no pressure to select one or another. On the other hand, without
flexibility, respect and accommodation, religious differences may become a source
of conflict and resentment."

Saundra Heller pioneered the development of "Stepping Stones—To a Jewish
Me," an educational program for children of unaffiliated interfaith families, and
has facilitated interfaith support groups at Congregation Emanuel, a Reform temple
in Denver, Colorado. Heller strongly advocates against allowing children to make
their own decisions about religious education. Children, she says, "don't understand theological or philosophical differences. Children perceive such a choice
as having to choose Mommy or Daddy. Thus parents have the serious responsibility of decisionmaking, a role they must not abdicate."

Heller advocates choosing a single religion for children in interfaith families. "Children need a foundation and tools in one religion, together with open
respect and acknowledgment of their other heritage. Without information, experience and grounding in one religion, a child has difficulty embracing or rejecting any religion. Cognitive developmental structure and age should dictate how
and what information the family provides about the other heritage."

Heller suggests that interfaith couples—before making a decision about
how they will raise their children—do a serious shared exploration of their two
faiths. She argues that couples need to seek out religious institutions to support
them. "Temple- or church-shopping will help your family decide on an appropriate religious institution. Participate in the service, visit the schools, speak with
the clergy and education director, ask many questions, know the school's policies and expectations, and be sure, if at all possible, that there are other interfaith
families. Discuss your reactions, needs and impressions with each other."

Learning from Children of Interfaith Marriages

As they grapple with the day-to-day joys and challenges of raising children, Jewish/Christian couples often wonder how their decisions about religion
and upbringing will affect their children once they've reached adulthood. When
such parents look for examples of adults who were raised in interfaith homes,
they find well-known children of intermarriage—politicians like Fiorello
LaGuardia and Diane Feinstein; actors like Paul Newman, Kevin Kline, Goldie
Hawn, and Carrie Fisher; musicians like Arlo Guthrie and Carly Simon. But
parents can also find thousands of less famous adult children of Jewish/Christian
marriages. And who better to instruct and advise concerned interfaith parents
than children who have been raised in similar situations?

The issue of identity—religious, cultural, and personal—is a complex and sometimes difficult one for those who have grown up in Jewish/Christian families. Adult children have had to balance and accept their dual heritages in order to develop a comfortable and satisfying identity. In the process, they often suggest, they have struggled with duality, have faced occasional prejudice and hostility, and have learned to be open-minded and resilient.

The attitudes and opinions of grown children of intermarriage are documented in **Between Two Worlds: Choices for Grown Children of Jewish-Christian Parents**, by Leslie Goodman-Malamuth and Robin Margolis, an excellent collection of the stories of adult children of Jewish/Christian marriages. Goodman-Malamuth and Margolis found that 44 percent of the adult children they questioned identified as Jews, 29 percent thought of themselves as Christians, and 27 percent considered themselves "nothing," "both," followed a "third path," or professed no particular spiritual identity. Goodman-Malamuth and Margolis have found that the least stable and satisfied children of intermarriage are those who were raised with little or no religious education or identity. One such adult child expresses it poignantly: "not having a religious affiliation, nor even having been exposed to either Judaism or Christianity. . . has been one of the worst stumbling blocks in my life. It caused me embarrassment and fear as a child, and caused me to lie on many occasions. I don't feel part of anything. . . ."

For the sake of their children, therefore, interfaith couples should work hard to make a choice and follow through on it. Then children will have a foundation upon which to make future decisions and explore their own beliefs.

Becky Seashore, the adult child of an interfaith family, is now active with both a Hillel group and as advisor to an independent interfaith family group in New Haven, Connecticut. She offers the following reflections on her interfaith upbringing. "Our different traditions, whether rooted in family ritual or religious belief, are an important way of maintaining our identity and community. Psychologists tell us that respecting and celebrating differences is especially important within personal relationships, where shared intimacy can threaten to overwhelm individuality. In this respect the inherent religious diversity of interfaith families can be seen as a hidden asset in maintaining the balance between intimacy and individuality (and as my mom would say, having twice as many chances to celebrate everything)."

How Does Growing Up in an Interfaith Family Affect a Child?

David Steigman, a forty-something writer and analyst living in Alexandria, Virginia, is single and grew up in New York City. He is the son of a white Jewish father and a Black Catholic mother. "Although I was raised as a Reform Jew," reflects Steigman, "my parents ensured that I, from an early age, knew about other cultures. I had a wide circle of friends from many groups, and trips to museums formed a regular part of my upbringing. My immediate family celebrated all the Jewish holidays, but we also celebrated Christmas and other Christian holidays with my Christian relatives.

"These family ties were important, because they helped give me a strong sense of who I was. . . . Because of my background, I judge people as individuals, not as members of groups.

"My advice to a couple in an interfaith marriage would be to raise any children in one faith, but make sure they know about both their heritages. Raising a child in one faith will give him or her a religious anchor. But exposing a child to both backgrounds, and explaining how and why the parents made their decision, could avoid awkward questions at a later date. Parents should also be aware that their children might, at some stage, develop their own religious identity. Hopefully parents can see this as a sign of growth. "

Another adult child of interfaith marriage, Cheryl Gavard Heinmiller lives with her husband in Elgin, Illinois. She was raised by a Catholic father and an Orthodox Jewish mother. "It was decided that I would be given a name in temple and raised Jewish, since at the time it was felt that the mother was the one to oversee religious upbringing. But it was also decided that if I ever chose to convert to Catholicism, that too would be accepted. So started my knowledge of both religions.

"I am now married to a wonderful man who is not Jewish, but was brought up knowing all the different faiths. So we decided that we would observe both Jewish and Christian holidays, and in fact we celebrate all holidays. Considering all of the problems that one can face in an interfaith relationship, I guess I am one of the lucky ones. I have faced the challenges head on and been able to deal with them, by listening to and learning about all faiths."

College-Age Children of Interfaith Marriages

Tamara Barbasch is a pyschologist and marriage and family therapist who lives in North Hampton, Massachusetts, with her husband and daughter. For her 1993 Ph.D. dissertation, she interviewed ten students who had been raised in Jewish/Christian families.

The college years can be a unique and important time for children of intermarriage, many of whom spend their first real taste of independence exploring their spiritual options and testing local religious institutions. The students Barbasch interviewed gave widely varying descriptions of their religious and ethnic identities. One young woman said, "I'm a little bit of everything." Another female student described herself as "an atheist who's a Unitarian who comes from a Jewish/Christian intermarriage and who recognizes both parts of that heritage."

Yet another said, "I guess I would say I'm Jewish by birth, Christian by upbringing, and Taoist by choice!"

One of the male students asserted, "I wasn't confused about [my identity]. . . . I am Jewish. . . . I consider [myself] more of an ethnic Jew. I can identify [with] more of who a Jew is, not what he believes or how he believes it, but his ethnicity."

Another student responded, "Legitimately, I'm Presbyterian. I was baptised Presbyterian, but my father's Jewish and my mother's Christian and I celebrate both. . . . My identity, . . . if people want to draw the line, [is] Presbyterian and Christian. But . . . my heritage [and] my beliefs are Judeo-Christian because of my experiences in both of them."

Barbasch asked the students about factors which had affected their religious and ethnic identity development. All ten interviewees stressed the relationships they have had with their families. Four highlighted a positive relationship with a particular parent, where identification with that parent was followed by a stronger identification with that parent's heritage and religious practice. In most of these cases, one parent was more communicative than the other about his/her religious and ethnic background, feelings and spiritual needs. When participants mentioned a contrasting lack of communication with the other parent, they expressed sadness and a sense of loss over the missed opportunity to learn about and share in that parent's heritage.

Family Matters

Extended family, particularly grandparents, also played a significant role in the identity development of the interviewees. Eight of the ten described how they had developed strong positive or negative associations with Judaism or Christianity as a result of feelings of closeness with or estrangement from extended family.

Participants valued parental harmony—parents who celebrated one another's different traditions, accomodated one another's different practical and emotional needs, and accepted one another's spiritual choices. The students underscored the importance of compromise, cultural exchange and shared values. They claimed that the presence or absence of such qualities had been the underlying reason for the success or failure of their parents' marriage, and had played a large role in determining whether they experienced their dual heritage as a cultural advantage or disadvantage.

Seven of the ten mentioned the importance of their parent's ability or inability to accept their own spiritual choices, whether or not those choices were in line with that parent's religious heritage. They emphasized how their parents did or did not communicate unconditional love and acceptance and how this affected their self-confidence and identity development. Several mentioned the opportunity to explore both Jewish and Christian heritages as important for interfaith parents to offer their children if they wish them to feel positively about themselves and their dual-heritage identity.

The Good and the Bad

The ten participants were asked about the advantages and disadvantages of having a dual heritage. All cited a greater awareness of multicultural issues and a greater appreciation, respect, tolerance and acceptance of diverse beliefs and differences in others. They believed themselves to have open minds and empathetic feelings for others different from themselves and for those having minority status in a majority culture. They agreed with the idea that they live on the edge of two cultures, feeling equally at home in both.

Half of the participants claimed to feel little or no confusion about who they are, what they believe, and where they belong. The other half admitted to feeling or having felt confused and conflicted, at times, as they struggled with a process of sorting out their complex identity. Some asserted that one individual can hold the beliefs or practice the traditions of more than one religion without necessarily feeling them to be in conflict. Some made a distinction between their current religious identification and their heritage. In the latter cases, however, participants continued to maintain a sense of connection with both of their heritages, usually by celebrating major holidays with family; most planned to continue this celebration with their own future children.

Eight of the ten participants specifically argued that children of interfaith marriage should be exposed to both of their heritages. Most agreed that children of interfaith marriage need to learn as much as possible about both of their cultural backgrounds. Although some admitted to the potential pitfall of confusion, they maintained that the price is worth paying for a sense of wholeness and an integrated identity. Without exposure to both their Jewish and Christian roots, they may always feel that a part of them is lost or missing. Even when an interfaith couple has chosen to raise children in one particular faith, they asserted, the couple should be certain to educate those children regarding all of what is rightfully part of their heritage and identity. They also stressed the difference between exposing and imposing religion on children, emphasizing that interfaith parents may need to be particularly sensitive to the dual-heritage child's need for religious freedom of choice.

Barbasch concludes that, "Parents, families, and family therapists may wish to note that children of intermarriage tend to crave and need a great deal of communication and spiritual guidance from their families, especially in the form of close, expressive, and educational relationships with parents and grandparents. Although efforts to dominate or control a child's religious preferences appear to be less successful, efforts to guide and influence tend to be praised as crucial to their ability to learn about what feels right and comfortable to them. The finding that relationships with grandparents and other extended family members may play an important role in positive identity formation also implies that parents take care to encourage and nurture positive relationships between their children and extended families, resolving tensions and conflicts if necessary to ensure that these relationships flourish."

Involving Grandparents in Your Decision

Barbasch's research clearly indicates the important place that grandparents hold in interfaith families. Children are very young when they begin to wonder and ask questions of their elders about the complexities and enigmas of their world.

Often these questions are asked of grandparents, leading to a deep and unique spiritual bond between grandchildren and their parents' parents. In interfaith families, when parents are trying to share with their children different or multiple faith perspectives, the cementing of this intergenerational bond requires extra attention and sensitivity. Interfaith grandparents can still serve as very important spiritual mentors, building relationships on a foundation of unconditional love and emphasizing their similarities with their grandchildren rather than their differences.

"In a world of change and challenge on a planet where our life-friendly environment is threatened, children especially need the security of continuity to help them face the future with confidence," write Drs. Robert A. Aldrich and Glenn Austin in **Grandparenting for the 90s**. "They also need the knowledge and wisdom which grandparents can impart, the history of both personal and community achievements and errors. . . . Children absorb the lessons of the past through the ancestral roots which their grandparents represent."

Grandparents of interfaith children are uniquely positioned to model their own clear beliefs and to provide unconditional support for their grandchildren as they grapple with questions of religious identity. Evelyn Maxwell is a registered nurse in Salina, Kansas, and a United Methodist grandmother of two Jewish children. "Grandpa and I have both taught Sunday School and believe that religious study is very important. We quiz the grandchildren on what they learn at *shul* [temple] and have fun seeing who remembers the stories of the patriarchs best as we discuss how to interpret them. Their father invariably gets the Hebrew Bible out and gives us the final version from the Hebrew itself.

"Our own Sunday School presentations have been enriched by what we learn from them about Jewish history, traditions, feasts, current beliefs, and the meaning of Hebrew words and concepts such as *shalom* [wholeness], *hen* [grace], and *hesed* [kindness].

"My son-in-law and I used to discuss our differences in religious teachings. Then he asked me to read the scriptures for what they say. When I began reading the scripture for what it says rather than for what I had been taught as a child, many of my own views began to change, so that now I am actually more comfortable with my beliefs and sure of what I believe on a scriptural basis.

"When gift-giving time comes in December, the grandchildren and their parents receive Hanukkah gifts from us, wrapped in blue instead of red and green. If they are at our house, we still have our tree downstairs and the star in the upstairs window. We forgo the creche and, instead, I get out the menorah so the children can light the candles. Our daughter graciously gave us the proper menorah and brings the candles for each visit.

"One of my greatest joys was being invited to attend the children's worship service with them at their synagogue last summer and being able to help hold high the shawl that covered the children as they read from the Torah. I loved to sing with them the splendid traditional songs of praise to our Heavenly Father. I've heard no finer praises in any charismatic Christian service I have ever attended."

Patricia Silver, the Jewish grandmother of seven interfaith children, lives in Great Neck, Long Island. All three of her children married Christians. "Our friends through the years have come from school, work, college, and neighborhoods. No one ever counted to see how many were black, white or oriental. They were just people we liked and with whom we felt at ease. We thus prepared our children to like and trust all people. This was brought home to me by a neighbor who stopped me on the street, having heard that all of our children had married. Her first question was, 'Did they marry Jews?' When I said no, she informed me that it was my fault. 'You didn't teach them that everyone else was the enemy.'

"She was right. We had not done that. I still think—no, I know—our decision was right. All seven of our grandchildren are children of a 'dual heritage,' to use a term my husband coined. It certainly is better than being half Jewish and half Christian—I always wanted to know if you divided the children longitudinally or latitudinally. Our grandchildren are at ease within their own skins. They know who they are. Three of them are being brought up in Reform Judaism, one is a Unitarian, and the other three belong to no group, as I did when I was a child.

"It's a big, wide, wonderful world out there, with many serious concerns. In my opinion, when we are all children of a dual human heritage, we can concentrate on more earthshaking things."

Edith S. Engel, Jewish grandmother of two Jewish and two Catholic children, is co-leader of a support group for grandparents in families divided by divorce in Scarsdale, New York. She advises grandparents of interfaith children to "keep an open mind and be tolerant. What counts is connecting with your grandchildren spiritually as well as physically. Rather than focusing on the differences, appreciate those things you share with your grandchildren. And never stop reaching out.

"As grandparents we were not at all concerned about the religious differences, except as another possible form of exclusion. We knew that learning about other religions should not be a threat, assuming that one's own religious affiliation is well grounded."

When asked how grandparents of interfaith children can be involved in their grandchildrens' lives but not seem to be interfering, Dr. Glenn Austin, M.D., author of **Grandparenting for the 90s**, a practicing pediatrician and a former president of the American Academy of Pediatrics, had this to say:

"With nine grandchildren, my wife and I have had to learn how to get along with six sons- and daughters-in-law of varying degrees and types of religious faith. To have a close relationship with our grandchildren, we had to keep a good relationship with their parents. To accomplish this, we have had to adjust to the various personalities of our children and the friends they brought home and eventually married.

"Our religious faiths are not so far apart that we have to dwell on the differences rather than emphasize the similarities. And unless we learn to get along with our children and their spouses, we will have little opportunity to let our grandchildren know about our personal covenant with God. Passing on our religious beliefs usually seems to be best accomplished by example rather than preaching. Maybe that is why most of us at best only cope with listening to preachers or rabbis for an hour a week, some weeks. And while many of us tend to place great emphasis on the differences between our religions, we might remind ourselves that the Christian faith sprang from the Jewish faith, and both are bound together in one Bible. In the long run, we and our respective religions will be measured by the way we act and the results produced rather than by what we say. In the short and long runs, our children, their spouses, and our grandchildren will measure us more by our example than by our words."[2]

Research on Children and Religious Education

Interfaith couples today are living in an unusual time. Growing interfaith marriage rates have rendered their decision to marry less unusual, but institutional responses and norms have not caught up with the growing number of interfaith families. So, while families are struggling with decisions about children and religious identity, their institutions are struggling with how to respond to them. Often this leaves such families alone with the immense responsibility of shaping and nurturing the next generation's religious identity.

Martha Fay, in her book **Do Children Need Religion?**, writes that "Today, having it both ways is what one is entitled to; neither party feels obliged to jump ship; neither is prepared to demand such a defection of the other. Fairness, therefore, demands that the institutions bend, not the star-crossed lovers. . . . What counts is imparting a sense of the sacred to children, of teaching them that something greater than oneself exists. And that can be done by one religion as well as another."

Adds Lee Gruzen, author of **Raising Your Jewish/Christian Child**: "There are no formulas or models to copy, at least not for now as the dynamics of Jewish/Christian relationships are shifting so rapidly. . . . Our friends, families, clergy, the media, and especially our own children will offer the guidance and challenges that help our answers become richer and more sure. But I've learned that ultimately the touchstone is within each of us, and it takes time and talking and experience to reveal what it is that we love and fear and envision for our children's lives, as well as our own and those around us."

Slowly, religious institutions and granting agencies are realizing the importance of trying to understand the complex dynamics at work in the growing number of interfaith families in this country. In the past, anecdotal evidence was used by critics to constrict and condemn choices made by interfaith couples. Now social science research is beginning to emerge done by independent investigators whose desire to understand the dynamics of interfaith families comes not from a fear of or opposition to them but rather from a dispassionate drive to find out what really happens when two individuals from different faiths come together and create a family unit.

Many have predicted that children of such families would grow up to be confused, maladjusted, or faithless adults. But the results of this emerging body of research clearly run counter to these dire predictions.

In her 1996 Ph.D. dissertation, "Mixed Up or Just Mixed? A Comparison of Adjustment in Children from Interfaith, Conversionary, and Samefaith Families," Juliet Whitcomb examined the expected and real differences between children who had been raised in interfaith and in samefaith homes.[3]

Whitcomb writes that "The dramatic growth in religious intermarriage has been one of the significant social changes in American society since the end of World War II. Historically, there has been widespread and often vociferous opposition to intermarriage from religious leaders and social scientists. Even today, interfaith couples who consult with clergy members are likely to hear warnings about the inherent instability of interreligious marriages or the harmful consequences of this type of marriage on children.

"As a result of the increase in religious intermarriage, a new generation of dual-heritage children has emerged in our society. The National Jewish Population Survey reported in 1990 that there were at least 770,000 children of Jewish intermarriage under the age of 18.[4] While a substantial body of research has investigated the impact of religious differences on partners in interfaith marriages, much less is known about the children of these unions."

Analyzing the existing social science literature, Whitcomb finds "significant disagreement concerning the psychological impact of interfaith marriage on the children of these unions. Anecdotal accounts suggest that such children will experience greater social marginality, identity confusion and psychological distress compared to children from families where both parents are born into a common faith ('single-faith' families) and families where both parents have a common faith but one of them has converted to this faith ('conversionary' families). Thus far, scientific research has failed to confirm these predictions."

Whitcomb cites the four studies over the past 20 years that have attempted to systematically test the predictions of the anecdotal literature. All of these studies, she finds, "have found children of interfaith families to be generally well-adjusted and nonsymptomatic. All of the four studies have failed to support the claim that interfaith marriages have a negative impact on children's adjustment."

Whitcomb's study represents the first attempt to use data from a large, national survey to systematically compare the psychological adjustment of children from two types of interfaith families—nonconversionary and conversionary—to children of samefaith families. The data were drawn from the 1988 National Survey of Families and Households (NSFH). The survey, which consists of a sample of 995 families selected from the main sample of 9,643 respondents, is the first large-scale survey to include questions on both the religious affiliation of married partners and the emotional adjustment of their children.

Whitcomb's study of this data found no significant differences among children from interfaith, conversionary or samefaith families. No differences were found among the groups on questions related to children's behavior, emotional well-being, academic performance or the quality of parent-child relationships. In other words, her study contradicted the previously accepted anecdotal evidence suggesting that differences between parents are detrimental to children's well-being. Her findings confirmed "the results of more systematic research which has found interfaith children to be basically well-adjusted and nonsymptomatic."

Making the Choice about Religious Education

Parents who want to guide the religious education of their children must provide a solid, consistent spiritual foundation. There are many options for providing children's religious education available to Jewish/Christian parents. A couple can choose to raise the child equally in both faiths, genuinely encouraging and anticipating their future choice of one faith or an amalgam of both. It can raise the child either Jewish or Christian, depending upon the strength of each partner's religious commitment, the ethnic composition of the family's hometown, or the proximity of specific family members. Alternatively, a couple can either find a "compromise" religion that is neither partner's original religion, most commonly Unitarianism or the Society of Friends (Quakers); decide there will be no religion in the home; or decide to "work things out as they arise."

The options available to Jewish/Christian couples are discussed in the following sections, punctuated by parents who have spent much time and energy considering their own spirituality first, before working with their partners to decide on religious education for their children. Although it may feel like a lonely process, an interfaith couple is definitely not alone in its struggle to shape its child's spiritual journey. Many, many others are searching and struggling too.

Harvey Cox, one of this country's pre-eminent Protestant theologians, is married to a Jewish professor of Russian history. About the religious upbringing of their young son, Cox had this to say to the *New York Times* in 1988: "I think we're in a stage now in the relationship between Jews and Christians in which a child can grow up being part of both of these traditions without violating either one. He'll be raised Jewish, and he'll get the 'Christian addendum' to the Jewish story—that's what it really is, a 'postscript,' saying 'Look, we're a part of this, too.'"

Interfaith families who are informed and connected to other interfaith families can make the best decisions about their spiritual and religious lives. No one approach is right for every family, and there are no easy answers. But a couple who works hard to communicate honestly and search deeply will come up with its own right answers. Such couples can be grateful for the special intimacy and spiritual closeness that many feel they have gained from grappling honestly and deeply with these hard decisions.

Choosing a Single Faith for Your Household

Many interfaith couples choose to rear their children within a single faith. This decision is not taken lightly by such families. It is often based on years of search and struggle. The partner whose religious tradition is not chosen as the family faith must come to terms with the personal loss this decision represents and must give up any dreams of sharing a religious identity with the children. He or she must face the loneliness of being the only family member to practice that faith, of attending church or synagogue alone (or with a spouse and kids who are not members), and struggling to explain this faith to the children without encouraging them to believe in it. The partner whose religious tradition is chosen must accept the tremendous responsibility of being the primary religious teacher and activity planner for the family. Of course, in practice both parents are involved to some degree in the religious education of their children. And sometimes the parent whose religion is not the family's ends up taking on the task of educating children about a faith that is foreign to him or her.

Until recently, the decision to choose a single household faith has been supported almost universally by psychological studies and religious leaders. Alternative choices—such as raising children with full exposure to and identification with both faiths—have been roundly criticized. In the abstract of a 1991 article in ***Psychotherapy in Private Practice***, Dr. Aphrodite Clamar, a psychotherapist in private practice, writes that "children of Christian-Jewish marriages are psychologically healthier if they are raised in the religion of one of the parents rather than in both faiths or none at all.

"While it is important to respect the double heritage of children whose parents come from different religious backgrounds, such children cannot grow up with a clear sense of religious identity if they are not fully at home in either the mother's or father's faith." Dr. Clamar goes on to admit that "the literature in this area is meager; the waters remain all but uncharted."

Writes Rabbi Samuel Silver—a pioneer in supporting interfaith couples—in his 1977 book, **Mixed Marriage Between Christian and Jew**, "children are more comfortable if they grow up naturally in one religious environment and . . . are no more capable of deciding on how to say their prayers than they are on what to eat or what to wear in their early years."

Rabbi Jeffrey Salkin, co-chair of the UAHC Outreach Commission and rabbi of the Central Synagogue of Nassau County, in Rockville Centre, New York, agrees, and defends the Reform movement's December 1995 resolution to limit enrollment in its religious education programs to those children being raised exclusively as Jews. "Our movement has problems with the 'dual religious education track.' The resolution we adopted said we should strengthen our programs for interfaith families, helping them choose a religious path for themselves and their children. But we also said religious schools should not accept children who are also receiving formal education in a faith that is not Judaism. There are borders and boundaries to what we believe, and to what we will do, as Reform Jews. . . . We are simply saying that children need one faith.

"I worry about those families who have chosen not to choose a religion for their children. For the result is not a religiously literate child, not a religiously worldly child, not even a religiously tolerant child, but a confused child. There are many such confused children. Such confusion should not exist. The parents need to clarify that, even before they get married."

"It is irreponsible to expose children to both religious traditions and imagine that the child will choose one. Young children can choose their sneakers (with supervision). Sometimes, they can choose their meals (with input). Quite often they can choose their television shows—and even here I am less and less comfortable with unfettered pre-adolescent autonomy.

"But when parents expect their child to choose a religion, they are actually saying: 'Truth be told, I don't care about religion, and I don't care if my child cares.' Parents have a right and a responsibility to say: 'This is our home. This is the religion that we choose for you to follow. While you are in our home, this is the path that you will be shown.' That is not dictatorial; that is simply being a parent.

"Parents who expect their children to 'choose' a religion are actually asking them to do something much crueller. They are asking them to choose between father and mother. That is simply psychologically untenable."[5]

Meryl Nadell, a social worker and former director of the Intermarriage Outreach Service of Jewish Family Service of Metro-West, New Jersey, believes that "children need a solid, coherent foundation from their parents to help them develop a strong identity and confront the pressures of modern life. Parents need to take the responsibility for the religious upbringing of their children. They cannot leave as complex a decision as religion to their children. A single religion in the home, with or without conversion, makes a statement a) that the parents are in charge and are there to guide them, b) that religion and traditions matter, and c) that families can grow and deal with differences."

All of this is not to suggest that those who make the choice to raise their children in one faith have necessarily been swayed by outdated, unsubstantiated claims. It is rather to acknowledge that their choice is the most acceptable to the majority of professionals who work with interfaith couples, and that they are welcomed accordingly.

Choosing Judaism: Couples Who Have Made This Choice

Robin Cohen Anderson, a freelance technical writer and editor, works at home in Easthampton, Massachusetts. She is a Jewish woman married to a Christian and raising her daughter as a Jew.

When Anderson married a Christian with deep religious faith, she began to explore the Jewish traditions she had discarded after her bat mitzvah. "Because of my husband's sincere faith in God, I have come to find comfort and joy in my own belief in God, enthusiastically exploring Jewish prayer, observance, and study."

Anderson explains why she began to feel strongly about raising her daughter as a Jew. "Being Jewish is more than a question of choosing a set of religious principles. It is about being part of a people, wherever you go and whatever you do. To be Jewish is to be part of a world-wide family. I want to pass on my faith—not as a religion my daughter must follow, but as a rich resource for spiritual growth and ethical action. And I want her to know that apart from her spiritual beliefs, she is a member of the Jewish people, and can find her own level of participation as she grows."

Both Anderson and her husband "agree that, as Ashlynne grows older, she will decide on her religious and spiritual beliefs. But she will decide based on knowledge of the Jewish faith, not based on ignorance of it."

"We live in a Christian-centered culture that can be very dismissive of Judaism as a failed faith. For many years, I believed love, mercy, compassion, and forgiveness originated with Christianity, only to find that they are deeply rooted in and essential to Judaism. Because Judaism is a minority faith, I feel it is important to keep it separate. I want Ashlynne to learn about Judaism on its own merits, to feel that it comforts and inspires and endures in and of itself. So, on Saturdays, Ashlynne and I attend synagogue together; on Sundays, we all go to the Unitarian fellowship to worship as a family."

Judy Kass is a Catholic woman married to a Jewish man. She and her husband are raising two daughters as Jews in New Jersey. Judy remembers the discussions about children she and her future husband had before they were married. "We were both strongly religious, and we both agreed that we didn't want our children to be confused. I had had conversations with other interfaith couples who were trying to practice both faiths in their homes, and I had spoken with adult children who had grown up in dual-faith homes. These conversations convinced me that having both faiths in our home would be confusing for the children.

"It was very clear to my husband that he wanted to raise our children as Jews. I had been through twelve years of Catholic school, but I considered myself to be pretty flexible, despite the rigidity of my Catholic upbringing. So I didn't really advocate raising the kids Catholic. If he hadn't felt so strongly about it, I guess the children might have been Catholic.

"I suppose I am making a sacrifice on some levels, especially on a personal level. I do my own thing—attending mass, celebrating holidays—and sometimes it gets a little lonely. But I feel no resentment and am willing to support my family's Jewishness wholeheartedly. It has gotten easier over the years to be comfortable with this arrangement.

"Christmas is hard for me, because my extended family is not nearby. Our family doesn't celebrate Christmas in a religious sense, and this is hard for me, but it is a choice I have made. We do celebrate Christmas in a cultural sense, and we do have a Christmas tree.

"But my own family's distance makes implementing our decision to raise our children as Jews easier than it would be if they were on the scene. My mother is not very accepting of our choices. Every once in a while she gives me a hard time on the phone. She seems to feel that I am abandoning my religion.

"I am becoming quite educated about Judaism. It helped me at first to realize that there are quite a few Jews who don't know a lot about Jewish traditions, either. What I really like about Judaism is the cultural aspect—it's a rich way of life, wonderful for a family.

"My husband's extended family lives nearby, so we share Jewish holidays with them. We are getting more and more involved in local Jewish life. Recently the principal of the Conservative temple's Hebrew school, where my daughter attends, asked me—knowing that I was not Jewish—to be the liaison between my daughter's class and the temple's board of directors. The temple's openness to interfaith couples—and to somebody like me, who is not Jewish and does not want to change her faith, but who wants to be active—is encouraging.

"Our seven-year-old started asking questions early, about God, about death and heaven. She equates the temple with a church. She doesn't yet understand the differences between the two religions, but she does understand that there are different religions. She has been to church with me, especially when Grandma is visiting. Every once in a while she asks me if she can be Catholic, but she doesn't really know what that means.

"I feel really good about where we are with this process. It is something we have to work at all the time. If I could give advice to other couples, I would suggest that they try to lay the issues out on the table as quickly as they can, before getting married if possible. You need to know what the potential issues are. It's not an easy choice to make, marrying someone of a different background and religion. Love doesn't conquer all. Children will complicate things and test your marriage in ways you cannot imagine. Compromise is important, but it doesn't mean that one person always has to give in."

Renee Weisman Michelsen is a Jewish woman married to a man who was "brought up Lutheran, but whose mother is Jewish, so he has many Jewish relatives." Renee's parents assimilated into American culture and did not give her many positive feelings about being Jewish. "Being Jewish was a fearful thing when I was growing up."

When Renee and her future husband talked about children before they were married, she remembers, "The world of religion looked very different than it does now." The couple was ready to be completely neutral: to celebrate holidays— not in a religious way, but in an 'American' way. They would share the Christian and Jewish holidays with their respective families.

When their first child was imminent, Renee remembers hoping that it would be a girl, so that they wouldn't have to make a firm decision about whether or not to have a bris. Her hope became reality, and it was not until their daughter Sarah went off to nursery school, coming home with stories from her friends about Jesus, that Renee was startled into action. She asked her daughter more about what she was learning, and suddenly realized that, even if she wasn't provided with religious education, Sarah would nonetheless be affected by others' religious expressions.

Renee's husband, raised in the Lutheran church, was adamant that he did not want to be involved with organized religion of any kind. When she asked him if he would support her in providing their children with a Jewish upbringing, he was clear that he would not be willing to participate but would not stand in her way.

Once Renee enrolled her daughter in a Jewish program, there was a rapid evolution in how both she and her husband felt about religion. His fears of dogmatic indoctrination dissipated as he met other families facing similar choices. While she was still primarily responsible for ensuring their daughter's religious education, he began to feel more comfortable participating by driving Sarah to her Jewish school.

Sarah developed a sturdy Jewish identity, largely through her involvement in communal Jewish education. As he watched Sarah grow, Renee's husband agreed that she should identify as a Jew, as long as the family "did it all." They joined a Reform temple with a large percentage of interfaith families. The family now worships and celebrates together. Renee feels strongly that "institutions that are supportive and accepting have made a big difference for us. These institutions have increased my husband's tolerance for organized religion in general. If our temple was farther away or less accepting of us, I'm not sure that we would have been able to create a Jewish home." She advises other interfaith couples to "seek out the most liberal, accepting place you can find, then try it and see how it feels."

As she watched her daughter's Jewish identity emerge, Renee began to search for her own. She became friends with a Christian who helped her understand the meaning of faith. Renee "began to realize how important faith can be for a person, and how each of us needs as many resources as we can find for dealing with this world. I wanted Sarah to have faith as a tool for life. And I got it, too, somewhere along the way. If you had told me ten years ago that my daughter would have a bat mitzvah, I would have said, 'No way.'"

Last year the family faced a challenge when they didn't go to Denver, as had been their tradition, to celebrate Christmas with the Christian side of the family. So Renee agreed that they would celebrate Christmas in their Jewish home. Sarah was able to differentiate, calling Christmas "Daddy's holiday" and being able to share it with him. For Renee, though, "It was weird and hard. We chopped down a tree and everything—I did it for him."

Despite the discomfort and occasional marital discord, Renee speaks glowingly of her family's progress. "You have to do whatever you decide as a partnership," she advises. "Try hard to be open about religion. It may be quite helpful for you and your partner to seek an independent counselor to help work through the tough issues.

"You can follow your child's lead, too. My daughter just loved being part of a group. She really needed it. I never would have admitted that kids actually need religion."

Choosing Christianity

Leah Ingram is a writer living in Ann Arbor, Michigan, with her husband and their two children. Leah and her husband have chosen Christianity as their family faith. Leah grew up attending a Conservative temple on Long Island, while Bill was raised in a Catholic family, also on Long Island.

Long before Leah and Bill made the decision to marry, they addressed the issue of how they would raise any future children. In a group of friends and family, they explored the hypothetical questions involved in interfaith marriage, and from this early discussion realized they had many issues to resolve.

Leah's mother was raised as a United Methodist, and she converted to Judaism in order to marry Leah's father. So Leah was raised as a Jew but was exposed to Christian holidays and rituals by her mother's family. In fact, Leah spent Christmas with her Christian grandparents in Maine.

Leah's mother really tried to raise her in a Jewish home, but wasn't familiar enough herself with the rituals and the holidays to do a very thorough job. Neither she nor Leah ever learned Hebrew enough to use it. Leah considers herself Jewish, but she doesn't "love the religion enough to keep kosher, learn Hebrew, switch the dishes at Passover or light Shabbat candles."

Bill, on the other hand, has wonderful feelings about his Catholic upbringing. A history teacher by profession, Bill has been able to teach Leah about his faith and about religious history in an objective, non-threatening manner.

Both agreed they didn't want their child to be without a comfortable, rooted religious identity. They had grown up with kids from interfaith homes where both faiths—or no faith—had been practiced, and these children seemed to both Bill and Leah to lack a sense of rootedness. It was relatively easy for the couple to decide their home life should revolve around a single faith.

Bill explained to Leah why it was so important to him that his child be baptized and raised in a church community. Leah's response: "Frankly, I felt relieved not to have to pretend I'm fully Jewish, not to have to do what was expected of me by my family." She readily agreed to Bill's wishes.

So, when Leah was about six months pregnant, she and Bill went church shopping. They sought a church where each of them felt comfortable. They found a local Catholic parish with a young, down-to-earth priest who was warm, accepting and creative in his use of non-traditional forms of worship. They joined this church, and their daughter Jane, born in July 1995, was baptized there.

Leah still has qualms about the Christian symbolism. "I don't feel comfortable with the cruficix. Bill says he doesn't particularly like it either, but he tries to remind himself that it was the form of capital punishment available in Jesus' day."

Leah is happy the primary responsibility for religiously educating their children will fall to Bill. "Religion is not a big part of my identity. But I don't feel excluded by our decision to raise our children as Catholics. And Bill wants this responsibility."

She admits the decision has not always been painless. "Sometimes I feel a sense of loss. Sometimes I work hard to identify with the other Jews in a roomful of people. I cry when I hear Hebrew music." And, while she generally feels acceptance when she attends the local Catholic church, occasionally there are moments of discomfort. "I don't like that Bill can take communion and I can't. I don't appreciate it when the church sends me information on their conversion classes."

Leah is fully involved in the family's Christmas preparations, and she found herself quite comfortable the year she explained to fifteen-month-old Jane about the baby Jesus in the manger at her daycare. Leah understands Jesus as "another facet of religious history on which I haven't focused. I can understand Christianity the way Bill explains it. He doesn't believe literally, but rather in the Christian allegories and what they represent."

Their two families have responded in predictable ways. Leah's mother was quite surprised to learn the couple would be raising their children as Catholics. Leah's father and much of the rest of her Jewish family were offended and insulted by her decision. Bill's family, on the other hand, has been effusive and thrilled to know their grandchildren will be Catholics.

Finding a Compromise: Neutral Territory

Many interfaith families think of their choices in terms only of the largest groups within Judaism and Christianity. There are, however, less well-known branches of each religious tradition which are appealing to some interfaith couples, and which can provide a welcoming local community in which to raise interfaith children.

Humanistic Judaism

There are an estimated 30,000 Humanistic Jews around the globe. Humanistic Judaism is a historical but recent movement in Judaism for those who value a Jewish identity but seek an alternative to conventional Judaism. Barbara Griss, Co-President of the Colorado Society for Humanistic Judaism, in Denver, Colorado, offers this explanation of its tenets:

"Humanistic Jews belong to two groups: Jews and Humanists (not to be confused with humanitarians). As Jews they value Jewish identity, heritage and culture. As Humanists they embrace a philosophy of life that dates back to ancient Greece, where some philosophers challenged religious tradition and authority.

"Jewish Humanists are not fulfilled by conventional Judaism's heavy emphasis on God, the Torah, and prayer. They wish to integrate their Jewish identity with their personal convictions, and they want to use language that reflects these beliefs. Humanist Jews celebrate and teach about Jewish heritage in a meaningful way (without worship of the supernatural), and they affirm the right for all individuals to shape their own destinies through freedom, equality, dignity and reason.

"Humanistic Judaism challenges the assumption that Jews are exclusively a religious community and that religious convictions or behavior are essential to full membership in the Jewish people. . . . For Humanistic Jews, Jewishness encompasses the whole gamut of Jewish culture, of which religion is but one aspect. The Jewish people is a world people with a pluralistic culture and civilization all its own, including many languages, many beliefs, a vast body of literature, historical memories, and ethical values. Jews are united by social identification and ancestral roots, not by their belief system.

"Humanistic Judaism has a unique approach to intermarriage and conversion. Intermarriage is an American Jewish reality—a natural consequence of a liberal society in which individuals have the freedom to marry whomever they wish. Intermarriage is neither good nor bad, just as the marriage of two Jews, in itself, is neither good nor bad. The moral worth of a marriage always depends on the quality of the human relationship—on the degree of mutual love and respect that prevails. Humanistic Judaism affirms the right of rabbis or Jewish leaders to officiate at interfaith or intercultural wedding ceremonies.

"Humanistic Jews welcome all, regardless of their ancestry, who sincerely desire to share the Jewish experience, and who feel a love for and commitment to the Jewish people. The non-Jewish partner is welcomed into the Humanistic Jewish family circle and is offered acceptance and respect. The children and spouses of intermarriage who desire to be part of the Jewish people must not be cast aside because they do not have Jewish parents or do not wish to undergo a religious conversion."

The Jewish Renewal Movement

A relative newcomer to the Jewish scene, the Jewish Renewal movement is an international effort to revitalize Jewish religious and spiritual life. Growing out of study of Jewish mysticism, the movement recognizes a spiritual path as an essential aspect of modern Judaism. Distinctive features of the movement include egalitarianism, lack of hierarchy, preference for the *havurah* or fellowship as the basic form of religious community, openness to ideas and practitioners of other religious traditions, an emphasis on *tikkun olam* or healing the world, and celebration based on the Hasidic use of dance and song as religious expression. The movement has spawned 30 to 40 Jewish Renewal communities in the United States, Canada, Europe, and South America.[6]

A Church Without Walls

Susannah C. West lives in Ripley, Ohio. "I'm a partner in an interfaith family. Though I attended Methodist churches when I was in grade school, I gradually drifted away from traditional Christianity when my family started going to a Unitarian Universalist church. My husband, Dave, is the child of an interfaith marriage. He received little Christian or Jewish education while growing up, but he's always thought of himself as being more Jewish than Christian.

"We live in a small rural community where there are no Jews and no Unitarians. I often hear derogatory or slighting comments about Jews, and few people in town even recognize the names Unitarian or Universalist.

"Many traditional Christians put me in the same category as an atheist. In spite of this, we found a church that we could belong to—the Church of the Larger Fellowship, Unitarian Universalist (CLF). It's a 'church without walls'— its 3,000 members (about 2,300 adults and 700 children) are scattered throughout the world. Many are Unitarian Universalists far from a UU church. Some live in countries where it's hard for them to practice their faith in their own way. Others, because of work schedules, illness, or physical handicaps, simply can't attend a church.

"How did CLF help our family? When we became CLF members, my main desire was that the church would show us how to give our daughter a religious education that explored both her Jewish and Christian roots. The CLF lending library started us on our quest. One of the first things I received was a new-member packet of information about religious holidays and holy days. In this packet, the many festivals of Christianity, Judaism and other faiths are described, along with ways to celebrate with the family.

"It seems to me that CLF can serve other interfaith couples as well as it has served us. For some interfaith couples, joining a UU church may be the answer to their dilemma. Sometimes, however, for the Jewish member of the couple, just being in a church, even if it is one that rejects many Christian beliefs, can be very uncomfortable. But because CLF does not have a physical church building, it may not cause such nervousness and discomfort. Though I am not Jewish, I find that this is true for me—it is extremely difficult to attend a traditional Christian service. But I am very content with the worship opportunities CLF offers."[7]

Raising Children in Two Faiths: What Does It Really Mean?

A growing number of interfaith families are choosing to bring both their faiths fully into their family life. The UAHC (the governing body of Reform Judaism) estimated in the December 9, 1995, **Los Angeles Times** that one-fifth of the children of U.S. interfaith families are being raised with a combination of religions. The courage and persistence of these interfaith families is evident as they forge a new path for themselves and their children, despite the frequent admonitions of religious institutions that they "choose one faith" or risk subjecting their children to confusion and instability.

Perhaps the confusion of some children, whether raised in one or two faiths, stems from lack of effective parenting skills. When adults provide open, respectful opportunities for discussion, and when children feel comfortable asking questions and disagreeing, confusion is far less likely.

Critics suggest that it is the parents' responsibility to make tough decisions so that children don't have to choose, between religions or between parents. The assumption is that Judaism and Christianity are mutually exclusive systems. But in fact, the couples who "do both" can complement one another. And, with parental guidance, children can make informed decisions about who they are without undue confusion or struggle.

Some argue that children will feel the pull of both faiths in any case. "However we ultimately choose to identify, we children of intermarriage are born into two worlds," write Leslie Goodman-Malamuth and Robin Margolis, both raised in interfaith families and co-authors of **Between Two Worlds: Choices for Grown Children of Jewish-Christian Parents**. "We inevitably reflect both heritages, as surely as we have inherited one parent's perfect teeth and the other's flat feet. . . . There are no guarantees about our future religious or ethnic identities, no matter how they raise us."

The number of interfaith couples who are choosing to raise their children in both faiths—and who are willing to talk about their decisions— is growing. Brad Bickford, a clinical social worker in Washington, DC, reflects on the evolution of his family's decision to include both faiths in their family life. "My wife is a very religious and moral person, and her presence in my life has made me aware of some of the richness which a religious upbringing provides. My Jewish upbringing involved a boring Sunday school, bar mitzvah, and little discussion about Jewish or human morals on a regular basis. I stopped practicing Judaism except on the High Holidays, and yet I didn't give it up entirely because I felt a loyalty to my Jewish cultural heritage. I now find myself talking with my kids more about morals and my spiritual belief system.

"Our kids get an 'enriched' religious upbringing. They learn about two different types of cultures with unique rites, customs and languages. In addition,

94

they are taught by my wife and me to believe in God, to believe that people are moral and they should treat others respectfully, and to be responsible to help those less fortunate. On Sunday mornings I pick them up from Christian school and take them to Jewish school. Our sons learn that they have a common Judeo-Christian heritage which began in the Palestine area. They seem to have adjusted well to the split in schools. I asked them whether they felt confused about being raised in both religions, and both kids said 'no.' They said that they liked it because 'We get lots more presents, learn about and get to eat different foods, and it's fun because we get to meet a lot of new people.'"

Susan Berns has practiced law and is now a full-time mom of two daughters in Tarzana, California. She relates the following conversation between her daughter and a friend. "I was half listening while driving my eight-year-old Madalyn and her friend to soft-ball practice. They were discussing an upcoming Jewish holiday and her friend said, 'You wouldn't know much about it because you're only half Jewish.' My daughter replied, 'That doesn't matter. I'm not half and half, I'm like two circles.'

"Her friend didn't get it. Maddie was trying to explain that you don't lose part of yourself by respecting two traditions in one household, rather you gain a new 'circle,' a fresh perspective on life.

"Our family has focused on the meaning of living with two heritages, Jewish and Christian, distinct yet related, carved from the same tree, yet branching in different directions. We have attempted to respect both traditions in our home. We consciously refuse to accept the oft-heard admonition: 'You should only practice one for the sake of the children.' We decline to join any formal congregation but rather choose to 'home-school' our children every Sunday regarding the holidays, traditions, values and stories we want them to understand and love.

"If you respect your spouse's different religious tradition, you accept its worth as equal to your own. Bob, who is Jewish, has hauled the Christmas tree into our house and written Santa's responses to his daughters' heartfelt letters. I in turn have scripted Purim plays, prepared the entire Passover feast and sung Hebrew prayers over Hanukkah candles. Bob and I bend over backwards to participate and share in the other's culture. In our family, the principles of mutual respect take precedence over the exclusivity rights of any one religion. In our family, the two traditions stand side by side, hand in hand, heart to heart.

"When Bob and I sit down with Maddie and Jessica for our home Sunday school discussions, we focus on the moral and ethical ideals underlying each religion's rituals and traditions. I prepare each week's session based on a particular value, such as forgiveness, empathy, gratitude. We then incorporate Jewish and Christian holidays, stories and rituals into each discussion and explain how these traditions help individuals live in peace and lead more meaningful lives.

"Despite the prophecies of some religious authorities, my daughters are neither confused nor hurt by enjoying their dual heritage. At their respective ages of eight and six, they are more interested in concrete examples of their parents' care and attention than the details of theological arguments. When Bob and I personally take time out to teach them about our traditions and values, the lessons we impart weigh far heavier than any they would learn at school, church, or synagogue. They bask in our attentiveness to their spiritual needs and questions. They understand that each religion is like a different language, equally important, equally justified in communicating with God. They accept and enjoy each heritage precisely because Bob and I have not submerged one of our religious identities for the sake of the other. Had we done so, Maddie and Jessica might have concluded that the suppressed tradition was less noteworthy, less meaningful, less useful.

"I agree with my eight-year-old. I believe that living in an interfaith family creates a new circle of awareness. From our perspective, we see only the gains, not the losses. When Bob trims the Christmas tree, he gains understanding of traditions different than his own. When I light Hanukkah candles, I appreciate the beauty in a holiday I didn't celebrate as a child. When Maddie and Jessica watch their parents understand and appreciate each other's diverse beliefs, they learn that difference does not necessarily mean divisiveness. They know that people from different ethnic, cultural and religious backgrounds can live and work together in harmony.

"They know that peace between races, religions, nations and the world depends on the same respect, tolerance, and understanding they practice in their family every day. Isn't this a lesson we all need to learn?"

Carol Horowitz and her husband Larry have been happily married for 20 years and have three children. During the week Carol teaches science in a high school in Charlotte, North Carolina, and on Sunday mornings she teaches Sunday School at St. John's Episcopal Church.

"When Larry and I told my parents in the summer of 1975 that we planned to marry, they were delighted. The only question or concern that they raised was 'What about the children?' With Larry having been raised as a Conservative Jew and me an Episcopalian, this was a fair question. We both felt strongly about our respective faiths, and, in all honesty at the time, our reply was, 'It doesn't matter so long as they are raised as something.' We were 22 and 20 years old at the time, and kids seemed a long way off.

"We managed to keep putting kids off because of school, work, and then because of the unspoken question of which religion would we choose for them. We learned about each other's religion: I went to temple for the High Holidays, learned to put on a great Passover seder, and was more than happy to celebrate Hanukkah in the winter. Larry was a CEO (Christmas and Easter only) member of my church and loved to celebrate Christmas at my parents' home in Cleveland. He did, and does, have trouble with a Christmas tree in our house but tolerates it every other year when we stay home and my folks come here.

"Finally, Jenny was born. We didn't have a naming or a baptism for her, and it wasn't a problem. When Jeff was born two years later, I agreed to a bris, but not to his full conversion. Neither one of us was a regular servicegoer, but we have always celebrated holidays with great feeling at home. By the time Betsy was born three years later, Jenny was approaching school age and we knew that if she were to be raised 'something' we would have to start 'something' soon. So, we started both church Sunday school and temple Hebrew school.

"We made sure that the religious school teachers were aware of our somewhat unique circumstances and asked them to alert us if there was ever any sign of real confusion. For the most part, the kids handled it better than most people expected. We had always had sorting-out questions like, 'Grandma and Grandpa celebrate Hanukkah, but what about Maga and Granddaddy?' They never had a problem with the fact that their relatives only celebrated one or the other holiday, because everyone in our respective families respected and loved us.

"Church Sunday school has never posed a problem, although my kids feel slighted that they can't take communion. Following up on the suggestion of a former minister at our church, after I have received my wafer and Jeff his blessing, I give him part of my wafer. This helps him to feel included.

"Between church Sunday school, Hebrew school and Junior Congregation on Saturday mornings, my kids get their fill of religion. They have always loved the fact that they get twice the number of holidays that all their friends get, and they really do get into the rich traditions of both religions.

"Early in her sixth grade year, we told Jenny that she would have to make a decision after Christmas as to which religion she would call her own. This was not a surprise, since we have always talked about it. We gave her some guidelines to help her make a decision. We told her that she needed to listen to the prayers on Saturday and Sunday mornings and see which ones helped her to talk to and feel close to God. That's a tough concept for an eleven-and-a-half-year-old. One of the biggest things for her to overcome was the concern that by choosing one religion she was choosing one parent over the other. We had to constantly remind her that the two issues were totally unrelated and that neither Larry nor I, nor our respective families, would feel hurt by her choice. I had always told her that I would be as proud as any mother if she chose to become a bat mitzvah—which she did.

"On March 16 she became bat mitzvah. Having gone to the *mikvah* the week before, she made her Declaration of Faith before the congregation at the beginning of the service at her bat mitzvah. The rabbi was wonderful in his support and offered flexibility in the usual service to allow me to take part when appropriate.

"Jenny's interest in Judaism has increased with her decision, but that doesn't mean she has dropped her enjoyment of our family holidays and traditions. She, too, will be a CEO with her Dad, but she did get into decorating and hunting for Easter eggs a few weeks after her bat mitzvah. Who knows what the future will bring to Jeff and Betsy. Whatever it is, I know that we have been most fortunate with all of our dealings with family, friends, church, and temple."

Like Jenny, other interfaith teenagers develop strong opinions about their special situation as well. Matthew Campbell became bar mitzvah on November 18, 1995, under the guidance of Rabbi Arthur Blecher at Temple Beth Chai in Washington, D.C. In his synagogue, it is the custom for the bar mitzvah candidate to choose a topic about which he wants to learn more. The child then researches the topic and gives a talk at the service, presenting what he has learned and his own opinions on the subject. Matthew chose the topic "Children of Interfaith Families."

"O.K., a rabbi, a priest, and a minister walk into a bar . . . mitzvah. Well, that's basically how my story starts, except it also concerns a social worker and an author. You may ask, 'Hey, what do all of these people have in common?' Well, they are all experts I interviewed for my project on children of interfaith families.

"I originally planned on interviewing only kids. However, most kids have never thought about this and didn't have much to say about it. Often they didn't even understand some of my questions. In spite of this, I did reach several conclusions. Seventy percent of the kids I interviewed said that their family would accept interreligious dating, but only twenty percent said that they would consider marrying someone of a different faith.

"For the most part, I know I have benefited from being a child of a mixed marriage. I get to celebrate twice the holidays. I hear very interesting discussions and stories my Christian dad likes to tell on Jewish holidays. And I am lucky to have four loving grandparents who, despite their religious differences (and the fact that they are New Yorkers and Alabamians), treat me as well as any grandchild could ever be treated."

Adoption: A Special Consideration

When interfaith couples have biological children, their decisions are questioned by extended family and their religious communities. When an interfaith family wishes to adopt a child, they are bombarded by even more questions, from birth parents, social service agencies, and legal authorities, all of whom may ask them to justify their decisions about religious education. "Hannah" and her husband "Tom" (they prefer to remain anonymous) live in Chicago with their two children, who have always been told that they are adopted.

Hannah offers advice to interfaith families based on her lengthy quest to adopt children. "If you are in an interfaith marriage and wish to adopt, what do I suggest? Take a clear religious path and stick to it. This doesn't mean you have to choose one religion over the other, but you must be able to tell a birth mother that there is going to be religious direction in her child's life. This seemed to be, repeatedly, a theme for the prospective surrogate mothers and birth mothers with whom we came in contact. While the choice of Judaism may close out some options, I would not let this factor control your choice. For every person opposed to placing adopted children with Jewish/Christian families, there are people who just want a good home with a strong ethical and moral direction for their child.

"Don't wait too long! If it becomes clear after a few years that you're not going to conceive, start looking at adoption possibilities right away. It takes time and effort, and there's a strong antipathy towards older parents among birth mothers, particularly as the age for birth mothers seems to be getting younger and younger.

"Most of all, unless one partner has converted and there is only one religion in your household, do not expect traditional adoption agencies to be of much use to you. The market for adoptable children is vast and anything will be used against you, including and especially your interfaith marriage. On the other hand, if you are looking to adopt, don't give up hope. Be assured, it is worth all the effort and much, much more."

Implementing Your Plan

You and your spouse have agreed and argued, shared and learned, cajoled and compromised. And you've come up with a basic plan for your interfaith children's religious upbringing. How do you put that plan into action? What are some of the key components of a solid spiritual education?

Religious education is a lifelong process, not one that begins and ends with Sunday school classes or cathecism. As parents, we can serve as guides for the beginning of that lifelong journey, with the understanding that all too soon our children will be ready to guide themselves.

Some interesting figures on religious upbringing come from pyschologist Evan Nelson, author of a 1991 doctoral dissertation studying interfaith couples' marital satisfaction.[8] In his study, Nelson found that about three-quarters of the couples began planning for the religious upbringing of their children before they were married, but only half said that they were still following this initial childrearing plan. And there were many couples who indicated that their plan was still evolving. Stressing that a child's religious identity forms over time, Nelson suggests that interfaith parents try to be flexible enough regarding their early decisions about religious education that they can adapt to their child's changing needs.

What's Important When Teaching Children About Religion?

The Rev. Roberta Nelson is one of the ministers at Cedar Lane Unitarian Church in Bethesda, Maryland, and author of several religious education curricula for children and parents. She suggests that it is essential for parents to be open to questions and flexible about changing their opinions. "Children who grow up in families where searching and questioning are accepted will usually ask more questions and will own their religious journey. . . . The home environment must be one of openness and trust in the religious search. Our young people need to know of our search, our faith, our spiritual strivings, if they are to have a foundation on which to build their own religious journey. As we become more confident about what we believe and for what we are searching, we become more creative in our dialogues with children and youth."

Tips for Interfaith Parents

David Heller, Ph.D., author of **Talking to Your Child About God: A Book for Families of All Faiths**, offers some specific tips that parents of different religions may wish to discuss with each other, and with their children. No matter what your personal and family faith choices, Heller's advice can be helpful. Among his ideas are the following:

- Be careful not to provide a cloudy or ill-defined set of moral values. Be specific and unequivocally clear about what you believe.
- Do you think that God has a special purpose in bringing you together as a couple? If so, be candid about what that purpose is. Tell your child explicitly about your reasons for being together. For example, you might say to your child: "God helped us find each other so that we could have you, and also so that we could bring together people of different religions."
- Ask your child what religion s/he will be when s/he is your present age. Find out the basis for that choice, because that may be an indication of your child's present view of religion.
- Refresh your own memory for the reasons behind major beliefs and rituals in your tradition, even if you choose not to adhere to them. That way you will be well-equipped to explain things to your child.
- Invite both sets of grandparents over for dinner if possible. Encourage everyone to talk freely about their backgrounds. A collective dinner can

help your child integrate the ideas of both families and traditions.
- Apply your situation to the importance of religious beliefs. Let it allow you and your child to take God more seriously than you might otherwise.

CHAPTER SEVEN

When Should You Expect the Big Questions?

Aside from a couple's wedding planning (see Chapter Three) and the annual questions around the winter and spring holidays (see Chapter Five), interfaith families can generally expect to be confronted by challenging decisions around the major life-cycle events of their family life. Rites of passage can be a very special vehicle for celebration and commemoration of the importance of faith and family. When a baby is born, when a child comes of age, when someone in the family decides to convert to another faith, and when someone in the family dies—all of these events can precipitate questions and re-negotiating. Early in their relationship, an interfaith couple should consider each of these life-cycle events, from "bristening" to "barfirmation," and discuss how they might handle them. Rachel and Paul Cowan, an interfaith couple when they wrote the book **Mixed Blessings: Overcoming the Stumbling Blocks in an Interfaith Marriage** in 1987, call such significant life-cycle events "time bombs," which can explode unexpectedly unless a couple considers in advance how to diffuse them.

Celebrating the Birth of a Child

A child is born. His interfaith parents are ecstatic, in awe of the miracle of a new life. They want to share their joy with their friends, families, and religious communities. They begin to think about baptisms, brises, and naming ceremonies, and about how to fashion a ritual that will reflect their dual spiritual heritages. But in Judaism, a bris is supposed to happen eight days after the birth, and the parents soon discover the difficulty of finding a mohel or a rabbi who will participate in their vision of an interfaith ceremony. And celebrating with only a Christian baptism just doesn't seem complete.

Hopefully, interfaith couples will be thinking—long before an actual birth—about how they envision welcoming their children into the world. For interfaith families, the birth of a child can become an opportunity to reflect upon and define the family's spiritual direction. Parents who plan their infants' welcoming ceremonies share common experiences of struggle—with family, theology, institutions—and feelings of satisfaction and personal growth.

Real Life Examples

David and Patty Kovacs, an independent writer and a part-time high school counselor in Chicago, Illinois, weren't satisfied with the prospect of doing two separate ceremonies when their son was born.

"We took time to develop our ceremony—we did not follow the prescribed calendar of a set day when the bris or the christening should happen—and so we were able to examine the phenomenon of change going on in our lives." The couple spent time examining the existing rituals in both traditions. Both partners used this period as an opportunity to educate themselves about both Jewish and Christian symbols and rituals around the birth of a child. "We learned to toss out pre-conceived notions (i.e. that the water of baptism washes away original sin) and rediscover the true meanings behind the symbols (to a desert people, water was rare and was, in fact, life itself)."

David and Patty are a good example of how an interfaith couple can be flexible and open to change in creating and sustaining traditions. With their first child, their celebration took place nine months after his birth. "We used the context of the Baptism, and adapted the ceremony, adding some Jewish elements, prayers and symbols. It was performed by the priest who had become our close friend and mentor. By the time our daughter was born, we had gained the friendship and support of our rabbi. He and the priest agreed to perform a joint welcoming ceremony. Both ceremonies were in fact very similar. Our second ceremony was an adaptation of the first, written under the guidance of both the priest and the rabbi. While both were extremely meaningful, we do feel that the second ceremony seemed more complete, enhanced both by the inclusion of the rabbi and the spiritual growth that we had made as a couple in the intervening three years."

Janet Lehan Bloom, a teacher for the deaf in Northampton, Massachusetts, who lives in nearby Amherst with her Jewish husband and two children, remembers her second son's naming ceremony. "This ceremony represented to us an affirmation of our great love and gratitude for our children's lives, a desire to give our child a Hebrew name in memory of his great grandparents and a middle name in honor of his Irish Catholic grandfather, and a culmination of years of thought and struggle about how best to impart our religious and cultural heritages to our children. The ceremony was officiated by my husband's cousin, a Reform rabbi who enthusiastically helped us to put together a ceremony that would reflect our desire to give our sons a Jewish religious education while instilling a knowledge, love and respect for their Irish Catholic heritage."

The Bloom family's ceremony represented for them the culmination of many years of searching as an interfaith family. "It established our right as a nuclear family to make decisions that we felt were best suited to us. It gave an opportunity for my husband to share his memories about his grandparents as well as a vehicle to express our admiration and love for my father's sense of faith, family and spirituality. It also set the groundwork for the special relationship that has developed between Alex and his godparents."

Allan Grant, lives in Herndon, Virginia, with his wife Beth and son Michael. When Beth became pregnant with Michael, the couple had already successfully navigated a decade of interfaith issues. "We were always able to work around issues that came between us. We chose to have both a Christmas and Hanukkah celebration, a seder, and occasionally we lit Shabbat candles on Friday nights. Incorporating these rituals was easy, as we were adults and we could make choices that fit us. They never seemed to interfere with each other, and we could live side by side with our mutual beliefs."

But the imminent arrival of their child changed all that. The decision about whether or not to do a bris (ritual circumcision) brought up new issues for the couple. When Beth asked Allen to explain why they should have the bris ceremony which would put their baby through such obvious pain and agony in public (and then serve bagels and lox afterwards), Allen was at a loss for words. "Of course we would do this. It was something I never even considered not doing, and therefore my powers of logic and reason failed me. When we started to question the difference between a bris and a circumcision, we found ourselves coming from two very different perspectives. For me, there is no difference; for Beth there is, and how to reconcile these two divergent views proved to be one of the more puzzling aspects of this search."

Finally the couple decided to make a list of what each partner needed and wanted, and to examine and question each of their long-held beliefs related to the religious welcoming of a child. This allowed them to keep the immediate issue at hand: deciding on a ceremony which would fulfill both of their individual needs.

Ultimately, the couple chose to have their son circumcised at the hospital shortly after birth, to forego the bris and to have a naming ceremony instead. The couple felt that this decision gave them "the most flexibility in making other choices down the road."

"By having the circumcision, we could carry on the Jewish covenant and the need for continuity between our family and God. Further, if we chose to raise Michael as a Jew, this was a place to start. The naming ceremony also gave us room to make other difficult choices. We were already overwhelmed with having a baby and felt strongly that we did not want a large family gathering like a bris soon after birth. We could now pick a date eight weeks after Michael's birth for the ceremony and the party."

Beth and Allen wrote their own ceremony. They gathered ideas from Jewish prayer books and other spiritual or inspirational readings and meditations gathered from a variety of sources. "It was a time when we found ourselves questioning core concepts of faith. This stimulated incredible soul-searching and fostered new levels of closeness in our marriage. It actually became an exciting time. We were discussing things we probably hadn't discussed since college-dorm-all-night-marathon sessions. The sensitive and incredibly personal nature of the discussions was exhilarating."

Both Allen and Beth have fond memories of the ceremony that unfolded. "The naming ceremony enabled us to incorporate our most treasured rituals of faith along with our prayers for Michael's safety, health, and well-being. The ceremony was a meaningful and profound experience for all of us involved, and we are extremely grateful for the many opportunities it provided in coming to terms with questions of our faith and spirituality."

What Role Do Clergy Play?

Most interfaith families would like to include the presence of religious professionals in their welcoming ceremonies. Clergy who participate in welcoming an interfaith child are forced to examine the choices encouraged by their own religious traditions and to confront the limits of their institutions' liturgies. Often they walk a fine line between acknowledgement and acceptance. The Rev. A.J. Good, pastor of Community United Church of Christ in Champaign, Illinois, reflects on his involvement in creating a baptism ceremony for an interfaith couple in his congregation. He worked to write a ceremony that respected the Christian nature of the ritual while simultaneously including a Jewish parent.

"The experience [of rewriting the baptism liturgy] made me more aware of a growing problem. Marriages across religious boundaries are increasing. When both partners are devout it becomes impossible to choose one of the two faiths for their children. The parents then try to establish an atmosphere of openness to both traditions. In Jewish/Christian marriages both the synagogue and the church pressure parents to keep the children faithful to their own rites. No institution, however, gives public affirmation or encouragement to the parents' efforts at remaining open to both religions. As a result, faiths that claim to stand for tolerance and strong marriages become instruments for intolerance and marital stress.

"Rewritten liturgies may only partially address this deeply felt problem. However, [this interfaith child's] baptism was an honest statement of the religious reality he will experience. It was also a public affirmation of his parents' efforts to respect each other, and to rear their children in an open atmosphere while being faithful to their individual commitments."[1]

Choosing Names for Children

When considering the birth of children, interfaith families must also consider how they arrive at names. According to Dr. Arthur Blecher, a rabbi and psychotherapist in Washington, DC, who has counseled hundreds of interfaith couples, "Jewish/Christian families have certain additional particular issues that can present both extra challenges and extra solutions. The challenges arise from the fact that naming customs tend to differ between the two communities. Christians often name a child in honor of a grandparent or other relative, regardless of whether that person is living or dead. In some Christian families boys are given their father's first name. Most Jews in the United States maintain the European Jewish practice of naming children in memory of deceased relatives (or occasionally the memory of a close friend)."

Dr. Blecher notes, however, the advantage that interfaith couples have over Christian couples since Jews in America usually give their children both an English name and a Hebrew name. "Interfaith couples have double the opportunity to provide names for their children that will satisfy family associations. The Hebrew name is used only in ritual contexts, such as marriage certificates or synagogue ceremonies. It is somewhat like the confirmation name among Catholics.

"Interfaith couples can choose an English name that has associations for the Christian partner's family and a different Hebrew name that recalls a member of the Jewish partner's family. Of course, it is the English name that will appear on the birth certificate and all other civil documents, and most likely will be the name that the child uses daily throughout life. Nonetheless, American Jewish families—almost without exception—are very pleased when a child is given a Hebrew name that honors the memory of a relative or close friend."[2]

Coming of Age in an Interfaith Family

On top of the many challenges facing teenagers in the United States today, teenagers in Jewish-Christian families must somehow come to terms with their distinctive religious identities. "The job of the adolescent is to question, challenge, and begin to develop independent reasoning abilities," writes Joel Crohn in the very helpful book **Mixed Matches: How to Create Successful Interracial, Interethnic, and Interfaith Marriages**. "In single-religion homes adolescents will tend to identify with parents' beliefs. In homes with two religions or no clear religion, the adolescent will often either reject religion entirely or choose one as 'the best.'" Crohn goes on to suggest that "each child's path through the process of creating an identity is unique, and all involve a process of experimentation and change."

Crohn acknowledges that children's struggles to understand their complex identities can be quite difficult for their parents. "We can guide our children, teach them, and expose them to the cultural and religious worlds we hope they will embrace," he writes. "But no matter how carefully we orchestrate our children's experiences, as they approach adulthood, we can never control or predict how they will identify. Just as we have broken with some of the traditions and ways of our parents and ancestors, so, too, will our children create change with the new world they are helping to create."

One way to help ourselves and our children grapple with the complexities of growing up in an interfaith family is to work together on a coming-of-age ceremony. As with each event in the family life-cycle, interfaith parents need to take a fresh look at what it means to "come of age." "If you understand coming of age as a passage, a process of transition from one stage to another," suggests Hugh Sanborn, a campus minister and pastoral therapist in Houston, Texas, "then it becomes clear that a coming-of-age service is not intended to be a completion, as though adolescence ends one day and young adulthood begins the next. Rather, it celebrates the changes that are taking place in the life of the young adult and the parents."

Coming of age is the one life-cycle event in which the composition of the family doesn't change. There is no birth or death; no new family is created. It is perhaps for this reason, since the change is more subtle and less immediate, that the coming-of-age ritual is by and large the least considered life-cycle ceremony for interfaith families.

The work of an interfaith family to plan a meaningful coming-of-age ceremony is difficult and multifaceted. Parents of interfaith adolescents must ask themselves how much the ceremony they are planning is designed to help them with their own issues, and how much it will benefit and enrich the child. As Susan Weidman Schneider writes in **Intermarriage: The Challenge of Living with Differences Between Christians and Jews**, "after birth, there are a few other ceremonial occasions that provide opportunities for the interfaith couple to express how they're raising their children and what their goals are for them." She suggests that coming-of-age rituals for an adolescent boy or girl are difficult for a family to navigate because "the religious aspects of the ritual obviously have an intellectual impact on him or her that the birth ceremonies did not."

Unlike planning for a birth ceremony, where the baby is oblivious to the rituals and blessings, planning for any type of adolescent ceremony requires working with an independent thinker who should be involved in the process. Perhaps for the first time, family decisions must be made by three, not two, individuals.

What Are The Options?

Coming-of-age rituals for children in interfaith families are an excellent example of how Jewish/Christian families in the 1990s are truly on the cutting edge of new ritual creation. Neither a traditional Christian confirmation nor a Jewish bar/bat mitzvah fits perfectly. For children growing up with two religions, it is difficult and perhaps inappropriate to mimic a ceremony designed to recognize full membership in a particular religious community. So families often find themselves changing old rituals or creating new ones.

In **The Intermarriage Handbook,** Judy Petsonk and Jim Remsen contend that Jewish parents are more likely than Christian ones to push for their own ceremony. "The Christian ceremony is a statement of faith. Many of the Christian partners we talked to had lost their faith years earlier. They saw no particular reason to ask their children to make declarations of Christian faith. The Jewish ceremony, however, affirms identification with a people. The Jewish partner may have no faith yet still identify as a Jew. He wants his child to share in that identification."

A question many interfaith families may find themselves asking is why a Jewish bar/bat mitzvah ceremony seems so important to them, when so often they have been unable to find supportive, accepting Jewish institutions to join. And in actuality, according to sociologist Egon Mayer, only about 15 percent of the children in interfaith families go through the bar or bat mitzvah ceremony. There are no parallel figures for how many interfaith children go through a Christian confirmation.

It appears that until now the majority of Jewish/Christian families have let their children's adolescent years slip by without a concrete coming-of-age marker. Chances are that, as more and more thoughtful, energetic interfaith families have children approaching the teenage years, there will be a blossoming of new ideas and new ways of celebrating this important life transition.

A growing number of Jewish/Christian families feel called to create something new, a call heard by Nancy Nutting Cohen, a member of *Dovetail*'s editorial advisory board, who lives with her family in Minneapolis, Minnesota. Cohen worked with her daughter Katie to fashion a personalized, inclusive marker for Katie's coming of age.

"I am a firm believer in the power of rituals. I think that there's a reason that religions have come up with bar/bat mitzvahs and confirmations and that cultures celebrate the onset of menses and 'becoming a man' with elaborate ceremonies. There's something deep within the human psyche that longs to be expressed, celebrated, and affirmed at these milestones in life. This is what I want to express in Katie's coming-of-age ceremony."

As Cohen thought with friends and with her daughter about the ceremony, she found a beautiful rite of puberty in Marianne Williamson's book **Illuminata.** "The part that touched me the most about this ceremony is that the parents acknowledge they haven't been perfect, the community acknowledges it's handing on a broken world, and everyone acknowledges that the individual, even though not fully an adult, is no longer a child."

Sometimes it is an interfaith teenager him- or herself who provides the impetus for a coming-of-age ceremony. Paul Rosenbloom of Palo Alto, California, is one such teenager. With a Presbyterian mother and a Jewish father, Paul was raised primarily Christian as a child. Attending Jewish gatherings, remembers Paul, "was never quite as laid back as the Presbyterian potlucks. My earliest memories of Passover and the temple are negative. I was dressed in formal attire, feeling choked by my tie. At Passover I would sit at the table while my uncle jabbered away in an alien language—I could not comprehend at all what was going on.

"I was incredibly turned off by Judaism, yet I tried to respect it. Some time during the seventh grade I started to get a nagging thought in the back of my head. I wanted to have a bar mitzvah. The whole thing was inexplicable considering my past experiences. I felt as if I had something to prove. I realized that while I was not particularly crazy about religion in general, I felt comfortable with my knowledge about Christianity. I wanted to familiarize myself with Judaism. I was tired of being so uncomfortable about such a basic part of myself. The bar mitzvah presented an opportunity for me to educate myself and to put myself at ease with my dual religious status."

Paul's father was supportive of the idea, and he hired a Hebrew tutor for Paul. After months of weekly teaching sessions and practice, when Paul watched a friend become bar mitzvah, he was able to follow along in the service. "As I learned the rituals for the bar mitzvah, my father, a cantor, began to create the service. Things slowly began to take shape. During the summer following eighth grade I became very nervous, kind of like I had a big test coming up that I hadn't studied for. I worked hard. In the local cultural center, I celebrated my bar mitzvah before family and friends. It was an amazing service. After I delivered my speech and participated in a few other ceremonies, we had a party at the community center. I vividly remember the sense of relief and joy of that afternoon. I danced my shoes off.

"In the years that have passed since the bar mitzvah celebration, I have been able to think about all that occurred. During the preparation I constantly wondered if this was 'Jewish enough.' I now realize that it does not matter if other people approve or disapprove of the ritual. I did the bar mitzvah for myself.

"While I am not very religious myself, I have benefitted from the experience of going through the bar mitzvah. I am now completely at ease when I call myself Jewish. I am now able to understand (sort of) what is going on in temple. I have also realized that most people actually don't really know what is going on. They are just good pretenders.

"The bar mitzvah has opened a door for me. I now realize that if I ever become interested in religion, I can come back to the bar mitzvah as a guide. For a while I thought of the bar mitzvah as some sort of a binding tie to become completely religious. I thought that I would begin attending temple regularly. This was hard since I didn't know any of the youth in the temple, as I did in our church. I did not enjoy going to temple solely for the service. I have now accepted the fact that I am not a weak Jew just because I don't attend temple regularly.

"Through my bar mitzvah, I was able to become more comfortable with myself. The beauty of the experience was that I did not shun Christianity, I only embraced Judaism a little tighter."

A Multi-Cultural Bar Mitzvah

Some families are able to modify existing ceremonies so that they feel comfortable to all involved. This was the case for Olivia Mellan Shapiro, a psychotherapist in Washington, DC, who married a Hindu man from India. The year before her son's bar mitzvah, Shapiro was "filled with powerful hopes, dreams and yearnings around wanting to impart to him the best of my Jewish tradition, as well as having this coming-of-age ritual be an expression of the deep and rich harmony of my son's mixed ethnic and religious background, and a reflection of the wonderful intertwining of all his family influences."

Shapiro considers herself Jewish, spiritually oriented though not traditionally religious. "As my son's bar mitzvah approached," she remembers, "I was filled with powerful feelings: guilt at not having given my son more of a Jewish background; longing at wanting to impart to him what I loved and cherished about my own connection to my Jewishness; overwhelm and fear about being primarily responsible for planning this event (with the active participation of my son, of course)." Her son began private bar mitzvah lessons about a year before the event.

For Shapiro, it was important that the ritual be clearly Jewish. When the bar mitzvah planning began to include Hindu chants and a host of quotes from that spiritual tradition, the difficulty began. "What was beginning as a bar mitzvah service began to lose its identity for me." Shapiro was able to clearly convey the message that "I needed this to be a bar mitzvah first and foremost; it needed to stay that way for me to have a sense that I was imparting my own tradition and heritage to my son in this Jewish coming-of-age ritual."

Shapiro remembers that, in the end, the ceremony was wonderful—a true melding of traditions. "It truly felt like the ritual expressed my need to impart some jewels of my heritage to my son, while still respecting and incorporating elements of his father's Indian roots and connection to his own spiritual heritage and practice."

Another Way: Services for the Unaffiliated

Shapiro is one of a growing number of interfaith families electing to use the services of a private tutor to prepare for their child's bar or bat mitzvah. Many interfaith families want their adolescent child to have the Jewish experience of a bar/bat mitzvah, but they are unable to find a synagogue with which they feel comfortable. Cantor Helen Leneman, an independent cantor (unaffiliated with any given synagogue), and a specialist in bar/bat mitzvah education with an M.A. in Judaic Studies from Hebrew Union College, offers an alternative: individualized, meaningful preparation to help, in her words, "make the rite of passage right!"

Leneman offers a variety of services, including private and/or group instruction leading to a personalized ceremony. Her goal is to make bar/bat mitzvah preparation and the ceremony itself meaningful for children and for their families.

Leneman reflects on why some interfaith families choose not to join a synagogue and to use her preparation services instead. Some families, she notes, "do not feel welcome in a mainstream synagogue. This is not universally true, but many synagogues do ostracize such families either overtly or subtly."

"I think these families are drawn to my approach because I am very non-dogmatic, non-judgmental and accepting. My approach to Judaism is cultural/historical. I am at heart an educator, and my urge to educate goes well beyond my course of lessons with the students. I am constantly explaining and answering parents' questions. During the service at which I officiate to celebrate the child's becoming bar or bat mitzvah, I explain the historical and cultural background of each part of the service. Many non-Jewish people who attend these services have thanked me for my explanations—as have many Jewish participants!"

Leneman explains prayers and their place and importance to the service, and she suggests both modern and ancient texts to enhance the service. She helps all her families prepare a personalized service booklet, containing all the essential Hebrew prayers of the service, along with selected English readings. Leneman sees the "ceremony as a wonderful time for families and friends to bond. It is also a particularly joyous opportunity for the child to shine, and to attain a rare sense of self-esteem. Christians and Jews can share in all these feelings; the service is different for Jews because Jewish participants have the sense of identity that will be absent for Christians. But I do not focus on differences."

Leneman recommends that interfaith families considering a bar/bat mitzvah service for their child check out synagogues well ahead of time—by fourth grade. Ask forthright questions about the synagogue's policy on interfaith families; try to get it in writing. "Try to get a sense of the underlying message: is it welcoming or withholding? Go with your gut feeling more than with official policy statements."[3]

Conversion to A Spouse's Faith: Who Chooses It and Why

Another complex and emotional issue that some interfaith couples face at some point in their relationship is the question of conversion. At least one partner has probably been asked about the possibility of conversion to the religion of his or her spouse. While many Jewish and Christian congregations are moving toward an openness that decreases institutional pressure to convert before a wedding, some less liberal denominations and a great number of families still encourage—subtly or not—the conversion of a prospective spouse. How do interfaith couples respond to such pressure? Perhaps they dismiss the questions without thought. Maybe the pressure to convert disappoints or angers an interfaith couple who has spent time and energy discussing its commitment to both of the two faiths it has brought together. Or perhaps the question leads to serious reflection and an eventual decision by one partner to convert.

According to a 1988 survey conducted by the National Opinion Research Center at the University of Chicago, 36 percent of Americans change their religion; the most frequent reason cited is marriage. "Switching is higher among Protestants than Catholics. It's higher among Catholics than among Jews," notes Wade Clark Roof, Ph.D., professor of sociology at the University of Massachusetts at Amherst.

Lawrence J. Epstein is the author of **The Theory and Practice of Welcoming Converts to Judaism**, and has done extensive research in the area of conversion to Judaism. "Conversion is a process, not a single decision," suggests Epstein. "It should be done over time. The decision you make today can change tomorrow. Some people who were sure they would never convert ended up doing so. Others planned to convert, took a course, and decided they were not really ready to do so."

Epstein offers a series of suggestions for those Christians who have been asked by their partner or partner's family to consider conversion to Judaism:

• Don't quickly accept or reject the idea. Learn about Judaism by reading books, taking a course that introduces Judaism, attending Jewish worship services and ceremonies, and talking to a rabbi, your friends, family, and people who converted. Learn about the conversion process. Learn the problems converts to Judaism face, such as non-Orthodox conversions not being recognized by Orthodox Jews. Similarly, examine your own religious background. Know what you are being asked to leave.

• After examining Judaism, see if its basic beliefs and activities make sense to you. Remember that becoming Jewish means more than accepting a new religion; it also involves joining a people. Judaism has many cultural as well as religious elements.

• Discuss your emerging feelings with your partner very carefully. It is also vital to discuss your thinking with your own family. Don't hide from conflicting feelings; they are natural. Many people who converted told me they maintained extremely warm memories of their early family life, including Christmas memories. Some converts save Christian mementos from their childhood. That is, of course, understandable. Becoming Jewish does not mean that you must give up your memories or your attachment to your family. But becoming Jewish will include beliefs that inevitably conflict with ones you were brought up with, such as a belief in the divinity of Jesus.

• Make a list of the positive and negative effects of both converting and not converting. Each person will have quite different lists. Probably no decision will be completely positive or completely negative.

• Don't convert because of any pressure. Don't convert for anyone else. Only do it for yourself, if you wish to do so. Most of those I spoke with were extremely pleased with their conversion because, for example, it brought them closer to their partner, because it proved to be a fascinating spiritual search, and because they found somewhere within Judaism a way of life that was enjoyable. However, other people felt like they were abandoning their parents, or felt hypercritical about joining a religion they didn't really accept, or had other reasons.

• Enjoy the search. Ultimately, deciding about converting is extremely stimulating because it requires a journey to the self, making those who are considering it ponder the large questions of the meaning of life and the significant questions of identity and relationships to others. Such a search can not only be enlightening, but it can also be enormous fun.

Conversion happens when an individual wants to enter into a new relationship with a chosen religious community. Conversions can happen when a quest for a new religious identity is successful, when a divine revelation changes one's life, or when the human bonds of family encourage closer ties and commitment to that family's religion.

Drs. Egon Mayer and Amy Avgar, in their 1987 study, "Conversion Among the Intermarried," suggest that there are three major variables that influence a partner in an interfaith marriage to convert: "(1) the strength of an individual's own religious commitment measured against that perceived in one's spouse; (2) the religious convictions of one's family of origin vs. those of the spouse's family; (3) the power and status of one side in the marriage vs. that of his or her spouse."

Some partners in Jewish/Christian relationships see conversion, especially just before marriage, as a hypocritical act which belittles religion in general. Others see such conversion as a way to pull an interfaith family closer together and offer a single religious identity to children.

Conversion is commonly very different in Christianity and Judaism. As Judy Petsonk and Jim Remsen write in **The Intermarriage Handbook**, "In Christianity, you convert to a faith; in Judaism, to a people and way of life." A convert to Christianity affirms God's forgiveness and accepts the teachings of Jesus Christ as the basis of his or her beliefs. A convert to Judaism enters into the covenant between God and the Jewish people and declares his or her commitment to the worldwide Jewish family.

Until the 1950s, when Jewish/Christian marriage began to emerge as a significant phenomenon in the United States, American Judaism made no organized effort to attract converts. Most branches of Christianity, on the other hand, have historically been committed to proselytizing and have welcomed the conversion of anyone who didn't previously believe in Jesus as Saviour. Nevertheless, the question of conversion burns much more brightly today for the Jewish community than for the larger Christian mainstream.

It is much easier among interfaith families to find converts to Judaism willing to share their stories than it is to find converts to Christianity. One obvious factor that tips the balance toward conversion to Judaism is that religion's concern with survival and population stability. More subtle factors include Judaism's emphasis on individual connection with a peoplehood (which discourages Jews from converting out of their religion) and the increasing tendency among liberal Christians to accept the truth and validity of other religions (which discourages Christian proselytizing and makes conversion to Christianity less important).

Despite these tendencies, more people have converted out of Judaism than have converted into it. More than 210,000 American Jews have converted to another religion, and there are about 190,000 converts to Judaism, or "Jews by Choice," in the United States today. From the 1950s to the early 1980s, conversion into Judaism increased very signficantly, more than keeping pace with the increases in the rate of intermarriage. In the last ten years, however, rates of conversion into Judaism have declined. Many in the Jewish community fear that as intermarriage becomes more acceptable, the motive to convert will further decline.

In the mid 1980s, approximately 28% of Jewish/Christian marriages involved conversion: 15% out of Judaism and 12% into it. At least one-third of these conversions happened some years after the marriage. Today about 9% of the Christian partners convert to Judaism, and about the same number convert out. Of the converts out of Judaism who are married (84%), nine out of ten are married to people of another faith. Two-thirds of those who leave Judaism are women.

Sociologist Egon Mayer wrote in his 1987 work, **Love and Tradition**: "The question of why some Christians convert to Judaism when most do not, and why so many Christians convert to Judaism when so few Jews convert to the religion of their Christian mates, draws our attention to the social characteristics of the individuals involved." Mayer noted that most conversions to Judaism are entered into by Christian women. He found that "those coming from a Catholic background are the least likely to convert to Judaism, followed by those who come from a family in which there was no identification with any religion." Christian women who came from families with a history of Protestant/Catholic intermarriage are most likely to convert.

115

"The fact that those Christians who choose to become Jewish are disproportionately women, disproportionately from backgrounds in which there is no distinct or exclusive religious tradition, and disproportionately people who themselves were unidentified with a religion before marriage, all suggest that the need for conversion may be felt more keenly by those whose identity is less well grounded in a religious or ethnic tradition than that of their husband or wife. . . . This formula appears to favor the Jewish mate in most intermarriages."

All but the most strident supporters of conversion in connection with interfaith marriage agree that conversion is not always the right decision. The process of converting to another faith is full of real joys and pains.

A person's religious tradition is a deeply held part of his or her identity, says Meryl Nadell, social worker and former director of the Intermarriage Outreach Service of Jewish Family Service of Metro-West, New Jersey. Nadell posits that, "after one's gender and race, religion is the most strongly felt marker of identity."

Conversion to Judaism

Lena Romanoff, Director of the Jewish Converts & Interfaith Network, and author of **Your People, My People**, converted to Judaism more than twenty years ago. At that time, there was very little information on conversion. She remembers that "Conversions were handled as quietly as possible. Intermarriage was considered a gross offense, and it was vehemently discouraged. However, if the impending union could not be stopped, then conversion was coerced as a last resort, with skepticism and misgivings on the part of the Jewish parents. Christian parents felt left out and their beliefs negated. The convert made the decision to convert with few resources other than academic information provided by books."

Romanoff, born into a Catholic family, spent many years of her childhood and early adulthood searching for a religion that she could embrace wholeheartedly. After being chastised for her many questions in catechism classes, she was surprised and delighted to learn that "Judaism not only permits questions, it sometimes even requires them."

Romanoff asserts that no one who has not gone through the process "knows the pain or joy that leads a person to conversion. Conversion requires clarity of thought and intent, emotional strength and determination. There is an invisible line between coerced conversion and encouraged conversion. The truth is that no one can sincerely convert to Judaism unless he or she owns the decision."

Romanoff sees conversion as a life-long process requiring a great deal of self-evaluation and honest questioning of one's current and considered faiths. "People who have converted for the wrong reasons have found that the process was empty and meaningless, at the very least," says Romanoff. "Converting for the wrong reasons can also make some people feel deeply resentful, bitter and burdened." She shares the story of Jacob, who converted to Judaism after being told by his fiancée that if he didn't, she would end the relationship. "He felt that he had no choice. His conversion was motivated solely by his love for his wife, not by his love for Judaism. He had set aside his own beliefs and his own feelings, even though he had once entertained the thought of becoming a priest."

Enthusiastically at first, Jacob tried to be a committed and practicing Jew, praying at temple and lighting Shabbat candles at home. But the conversion just refused to have the desired effect. He could not suppress his personal need for Jesus in his life. Living a lie was taking an enormous toll on him. He renounced his conversion. His wife felt betrayed and angry.

"The decision," reflects Romanoff, "has to be right for each individual. The choice to convert is seldom simple. It often is complex and conflictive, intertwined with the feelings of significant others. It is a choice which can only be made in a private moment of introspective thought."

Conversion to Christianity

Amy Krieger Rippis, a freelance writer raised as a Jew in New Jersey, made the decision to convert before becoming engaged to her partner George, an Eastern Orthodox Christian.

Rippis "was drawn to Christianity's emphasis on the need for faith" even before she met her husband. She reflects on her decision: "My motivation for converting was, undoubtedly, love. The Orthodox Church does not recognize interfaith marriages. Pulling the foundation out from under George was not the solution. My converting, I believed, would lead to a stronger marriage."

Rippis remembers that her family, though fond of her husband, wasn't pleased with the prospect of a church wedding. Her parents believed embarrassment could be avoided if the wedding were held some place far away—where relatives would be unable to attend. Her mother felt threatened by the prominence of the cross in the church.

Rippis remembers that "At the time of the wedding, my primary goal was to help my parents through the ordeal of seeing their only daughter get married in a church. Only afterward would I focus on my own difficulties. Although a nonobservant Jew, I was nonetheless steeped in the culture and heritage of the Jewish people. At the same time, I found aspects of Christianity appealing. How, I wondered, could I embrace both Jewish and Christian beliefs?"

After the honeymoon, Rippis' conversion became a bone of contention; the couple's frequent arguments tended to focus on religious issues. Rippis was often reluctant to attend church and found herself criticizing Eastern Orthodox practices. She missed celebrating Passover, "a holiday that holds some of my happiest childhood memories." After three years of sadness at that time of year, she talked to her husband. "I approached the subject with trepidation, as I didn't want him to perceive my ingrained need as an overall change of heart. His reaction was better than I expected. We agreed to incorporate Passover into our Easter celebration, where we believe it belongs naturally, anyway."

Rippis has learned that compromise is a big part of her conversion experience. She felt self-conscious wearing the cross given her by her mother-in-law, as if wearing it was "proclaiming one identity over the other. Plus, my mother admitted that the cross made her uncomfortable. I've resolved that problem by wearing the cross under my clothes, and in consideration to my parents, not at all when I visit them."

After years of marriage, many of the early issues around her conversion have been resolved. With time, Rippis has come to see herself as "a member of both worlds. I perceive myself as a bridge, a person who encompasses two religions, two worlds."

How Family Members Respond

For social worker Meryl Nadell, some of the biggest challenges attached to the conversion process are the responses of family members. While some new converts are accepted by their own family and welcomed by their in-laws, others face disappointnemt and lack of acceptance. Nadell cites the cases of Sharon, who speaks of a father-in-law who still calls her his "shiksa daughter-in-law" ten years after her conversion, and Cathy, who has yet to tell her parents she has converted to Judaism because she is afraid to hurt them.

No matter how clear the decision to convert may seem, the process is never simple. Cheryl Lawrence, a freelance writer living in Baton Rouge, Louisiana, converted to Judaism, her husband's religion, after a childhood of Presbyterian upbringing. Her husband Keith never put direct pressure on her to convert, but he had insisted from the beginning that their children be raised Jewish. Even though he is not religious, he feels strongly about belonging to the Jewish people.

Lawrence studied Judaism and practiced Jewish rituals for six years before undergoing the conversion process. "Conversion was a simple matter with our Reform rabbi. I later learned that a frequent criticism of Reform rabbis is that they make it too easy. Our rabbi required that I recite the *She'ma* and that I write an essay on why I wanted to be Jewish. The ceremony itself lasted maybe ten minutes."

One of Lawrence's primary reasons for conversion centered on her family. "I want my children to feel they are on solid ground, religiously. There are some couples who are able to walk the interfaith tightrope: teaching their children both traditions fairly, and even somehow explaining God in both Christian and Jewish terms. I didn't feel up to the challenge. Having come from a family split between the religions of the parents (and two Christian denominations, at that!), I wanted something different for my children. I felt that I could do a better job of raising Jewish children if I were Jewish."

Lawrence is honest about the mixed emotions she has experienced. "Although my spiritual life since conversion often has been uplifting and exciting, it has not been all happiness and light. I was in for some shocks." Her Jewish friends were not as excited as she had expected, often expressing surprise and puzzlement about her decision.

She also felt alone as a new Jew by choice. "There is a painful shortage of support and encouragement for Jews by Choice in sections of the country, including my own, where the Jewish population is small and generally not observant. A new convert desperately needs a mentor or a knowledgeable Jewish family to take him or her under the wing. I never had that mentor, and even now, when I'm in a group of Jewish women, I feel like I stick out like a sore Protestant thumb."

Lawrence's enthusiasm about her newly adopted faith grew old for her Jewish husband. "At first Keith was proud of my conversion, but as time passed, he grew weary of my exhilaration. He dislikes observing many Jewish holidays. He enjoys eating non-kosher foods and isn't about to give them up. He would prefer to attend religious services infrequently, perhaps just on Rosh Hoshanah and Yom Kippur and a few other times a year. Talking about God makes him feel ill at ease."

She and Keith worked hard to strike a balance. "We attend Shabbat services about once a month. I gently encourage Keith to get into the spirit of the holidays, but I try not to push. In September, we built a *sukkah* in our backyard and decorated it with our children's enthusiastic help. We held a wine and cheese party under it one cool afternoon. Almost every Friday evening, I prepare a Sabbath dinner, and we light the candles and say the blessings.

"But there are certain times—like Passover and Yom Kippur—when I feel overwhelmed by my lack of understanding, and I tell Keith that if he wants our family to be observant during these times, then he must take the lead. Generally, he does."

The Special Circumstances of Death in an Interfaith Family

The topic of death is one most of us generally choose to avoid. We prefer to ignore the unpleasant reality that someday we will be separated from beloved family members and friends. Yet, for interfaith families especially, it is a topic that cries out for discussion. The time surrounding a family member's death is always tragic and emotional, and if the complicated details of interfaith funerals and mourning rituals have never been discussed, it brings with it an unnecessary layer of confusion and painfully forced decision-making.

Perhaps the hardest aspect of dealing with death in an interfaith family is the conflict between contrasting sets of mourning rituals. Jewish and Christian approaches to death are quite different, and finding a common ground where both partners in an interfaith marriage—not to mention their families—would be comfortable is difficult. Susan Weidman Schneider, author of **Intermarriage: The Challenge of Living with Differences Between Christians & Jews**, cites the interfaith family's "conflicting loyalties—to the tradition of a deceased parent or spouse, and to their own needs for comfort in a time of grieving."

The potential conflicts are easy to spot, once a couple begins to look. Stoicism, a typical Protestant response to a painful situation, is foreign to Jews. The seven-day shiva period, when Jewish family members do not cook or go back to work, may seem excessive to Christians who have been conditioned to "keep busy" or "get on with life" as soon as possible. Jews generally put little stock in consideration of a life after death, while such a possibility is a central tenet for many Christians, so the phrasing of beliefs and philosophy for the comfort of all family members during a funeral service can be extremely hard. Even the seemingly straightforward questions of how ornate the casket should be and whether or not it should be open have quite different answers for members of the two faiths. Christians generally choose a more ornate casket and surround it with flowers. Jews are buried in a simple, unordained pine box. Christians usually embalm the bodies of their deceased, Jews do not.

In recent decades, some of these traditional funeral and mourning practices have become less definitive, as people look more deeply at the meaning of death rituals and adapt them to changing times and beliefs. Cremation has become a more popular option; answers to the question of afterlife are no longer taken for granted. This increasing openness will probably be helpful to interfaith couples who are forced to deal with the death of a loved one. Some couples may feel less constrained to follow religious traditions that are no longer the standard for their denomination, and instead will be freer to create the kind of funeral and mourning rituals that are most comforting to them.

Nevertheless, differences in culture and religious practice make it essential for interfaith couples to talk about what they want for the marking of their own deaths. If all of this seems morbid and you find it painful to discuss, consider the fact that you are helping your partner by easing the difficulty of planning should tragedy occur. By making the hard decisions now, you and your partner will be freed from the awful situation of being forced to make them in the midst of crisis later.

"For the survivor," writes Schneider, "having these arrangements in place in advance can mean the difference between experiencing the normal pain of grief or living through the additional cruelty of [details like] searching for an appropriate burial ground in an urgent situation."

If couples can be open and honest about what they want for their death, they will be helping each other plan, and they may come as well to a renewed appreciation of each other. Indeed, parents and children alike may realize that our experiences with death can be a tremendous resource. As Elisabeth Kübler-Ross, the world-renowned authority and counselor on death, wrote in her 1975 book, **Death: The Final Stage of Growth**, "death does not have to be a catastrophic, destructive thing; indeed, it can be viewed as one of the most constructive, positive, and creative elements of culture and life." She goes on to hope that her readers can realize that "all people are basically alike; they share the same fears and the same grief when death occurs. . . . In the decades to come we may see one universe, one humankind, one religion that unites us all in a peaceful world. . . . Through understanding that in the end we all share the same destiny—that just as surely as we are alive, so we will die—we may come also to understand that in life also we must be as one, aware and appreciative of our differences and yet accepting that in our humanness, we are all alike."

Through her work on death and dying, Kübler-Ross has developed a well-considered vision of a world where religious and cultural differences are celebrated, where interfaith marriage is expected and respected.

Mary Heléne Rosenbaum and Stanley Ned Rosenbaum, Ph.D., are, respectively, a practicing Catholic and an observant Jew. The deaths of their parents forced them to think about interfaith issues that—after over 30 years of successful marriage—they hadn't focused on before. In their words, "A parent's death can serve as a sort of trial run for the problems you'll face when it's one of the two of you."

Mary Rosenbaum reflects on the funerals of her father and Ned's mother. "When Ned's mother died, the ceremony was so secular in tone that we both felt religiously distanced. We felt more comfortable at the memorial service that preceded my father's burial. Though it didn't take place in a church, a local priest said a few words."

The funerals of their parents raised many questions for the Rosenbaums. Could they find a cemetery that would allow side-by-side interment of a Catholic and a Jew? Would Ned feel alienated sitting in a church next to Mary Heléne's coffin covered with a pall that has a cross embroidered on it? Or listening to the priest quote Jesus? How would Mary Heléne feel when some other family member says kaddish at Ned's funeral, because Jewish law forbids her saying it?

The essential question, in the Rosenbaums' words, is simple: "Will you, in short, be able to carry out the wishes of a deceased spouse even if they contradict your own beliefs? And if you do, will you feel estranged at the very end of your lives together? Or can your differences be the occasion for bringing you closer together?"

Legal Issues to Consider

One way to focus on your own answers to these questions is by exploring the estate planning issues facing interfaith couples. Dan Josephs, an attorney in Illinois whose practice includes probate and estate planning matters, is intermarried. He first realized the importance of considering issues surrounding death when he took his Jewish wife to his Catholic grandmother's wake. "When Abbe and I walked into the funeral home, I realized how uncomfortable she was and how little we had discussed our respective traditions' funeral customs. My parents and brothers were standing next to my grandmother's body in an open casket, and all Abbe wanted to do was to stand as far away as possible."

After that experience, the Josephses began to discuss their own mortality. They realized that "planning for your death and for your children's future after your death also involves looking at and resolving issues that are not encountered if you and your partner are of the same faith." Dan suggests that each interfaith couple consult with their local attorney. And he ofers the following tips:

- One of the first steps is to learn about and discuss with each other your respective funeral rites and the meanings of these rituals. As my wife found out, the Catholic wake is much different from the Jewish *shiva* period.
- Another task is to discuss with your spouse the type of funeral you want. This would include such things as, in the Catholic tradition, whether you would wish a wake, a Mass, an open or closed casket, a service at the cemetery, etc. In the Jewish tradition you might discuss the timing of the funeral, the type and place of the service, and the location of the shiva. You might also decide if you wish a particular officiant (priest, rabbi, etc.).
- Remember that your spouse may not be familiar with your tradition's funeral service. Additionally, some of your family members may want to become involved in the planning of the funeral service. As well meaning as they may be, they may put extra pressure on your grieving spouse to do things the way they are used to doing them. It could be appropriate to write out for your spouse a description of your funeral service. You should consult with your attorney as to the most legally effective way to include your wishes for the funeral service as part of your estate plan.
- Another way to help your spouse with the funeral service would be in your selection of the executor of your will. The executor is the person

who executes your will upon your death. Normally, your spouse is named the executor. It would be advisable to name a successor executor, who should be someone whom you both can trust to carry out your wishes. If your spouse has survived you and is acting as your executor, the successor executor can help informally with the arrangements. If your spouse has not survived you, or if your spouse does not wish to act as executor, the successor executor can make the funeral arrangements pursuant to your wishes. Talk to your attorney about how to reduce the stress on your spouse and everyone else and to let people know of your wishes with respect to the funeral.

- Another potential problem facing interfaith couples is the choice of a burial plot. Some cemeteries, if they have a particular religious affiliation, may restrict who can be buried there. Married couples usually wished to be buried together. It is best to do the necessary research when planning for a burial place. Your families may have burial plots, but you need to find out if those cemeteries can accomodate an interfaith couple.

- You must also plan for the care of your children after your death. One way to do this, in some states, is through the choice of a guardian or caretaker for your minor children. Since there are many different ways to proceed with respect to your children's religious education, you must be careful in choosing the person to fill the role of caretaker of your children. If that person will be entrusted with the care of your children, you want him or her to follow your wishes with respect to their religious education.

- You may be able to make your wishes known with respect to your children's religious education by including your wishes somehow in your estate plan. You should discuss with your attorney how to do so. You should also consult with your attorney about the legal enforceability of naming an individual as the guardian or caretaker of your children in your estate plan and the powers of the caretaker. These issues may become quite important and controversial if some family members are not comfortable with the religious education of your children. Discussing your wishes with your named caretaker and with your attorney will contribute to your plans for your children being fulfilled.

Josephs stresses the research, consideration, and discussion needed to prepare an estate plan. Because of the unique issues facing an interfaith couple, such a well-developed estate plan is extremely important, and will save unnecessary stress on family members at an already difficult time.

When Two Faiths Grieve Together

For one interfaith family in Boulder, Colorado, the excruciating pain of death came unexpectedly, when their six-month-old daughter Madeline died of sudden infant death syndrome. Each of Madeline's parents reached instinctively for their own religious traditions for comfort and guidance. Madeline's mother, youth pastor at a local Methodist church, turned to other pastors and church leaders for support. Madeline's father had been raised Jewish but had grown distant from the holidays and rituals as an adult. Upon the death of his daughter, however, he was overcome with a strong urge to incorporate into his grief the rituals he remembered from childhood. Part of his need came from knowing that his Jewish mother would come for the funeral and wanting her to be comforted by familiar rituals; part was his own desperate search for solace. With the help of a Jewish friend, he covered mirrors throughout the house and began the search for a sympathetic rabbi who would consent to being part of the mourning process.

Since the couple was interfaith and the child had not been considered Jewish, he expected hesitation or rejection when he asked for help with the funeral. But every rabbi he contacted was willing not only to be part of the memorial service but also to comfort and counsel the family.

Creation of a meaningful memorial service, one that would reflect the joy of Madeline's short life and the pain of her loss from both Jewish and Christian perspectives, was extremely difficult. But despite the shock and pain everyone was experiencing (or perhaps because of these commonly felt emotions), the process of planning the memorial service was infused with a spirit of support and trancendence of difference. The church choir director searched the Methodist hymnal for appropriate music and taught the choir members to sing a Hebrew blessing. The pastors and rabbi gave moving eulogies. The Mourner's Kaddish was recited, as was the Lord's Prayer. Amidst great anguish, there was obvious love.

Usually, when there is a death in an interfaith family, religious differences are transcended as people pulled together in grief and in support. Any petty comments or misunderstandings are dwarfed by the outpouring of empathy and respect.

In times of trouble, people cling strongly to their religious upbringings. We take comfort from what we know, what we were raised with. The old familiar customs of mourning and burial are a helpful crutch at a painful time.

This is an important lesson for Jewish/Christian couples. It is enjoyable and challenging to work to create a meaningful interfaith wedding or naming ceremony. But there will be no such joy or challenge in creating an interfaith memorial service for a family member; in fact, it will be the last thing you want to think about. Any time that you can devote now to thinking and talking about your wishes for your death will be well worth it for someone later on.

CHAPTER EIGHT

Where Can You Turn for Help?

Despite an interfaith couple's best intentions, hardest work, and most earnest discussions, there will be times when it will need help with sorting out the issues it faces. Interfaith couples should never think of themselves as alone in the struggle to create and nurture a satisfying and meaningful family life. There are literally a million other people in this country struggling intimately with similar issues, not to mention the millions of others—professionals and members of extended families—whose work and/or family life is impacted by the same questions.

Depending on their specific needs, interfaith couples can turn to professional therapists, sympathetic clergypeople, legal advisors, and other interfaith couples for support, information and practical advice. Sometimes a couple can find a local support group composed of interfaith families. Sometimes the help of a professional therapist is invaluable. Sometimes the couple must face the painful possibility of divorce. In this chapter, we explore the various options for help.

Independent Interfaith Couples Support Groups

Something exciting and unprecedented is happening with regard to interfaith families—they are beginning to organize themselves into local groups. From New Haven to San Francisco, Chicago to Tulsa, groups of Jewish/Christian families are gathering on a regular basis.

According to Egon Mayer, sociologist at Brooklyn College and director of the Jewish Outreach Institute, intermarried couples "need kindred spirits to share concerns about childrearing and the marriage itself." With this larger goal before them, local interfaith groups form for different specific reasons. Some are created primarily for adults to explore questions of spirituality and culture. Some have their roots in the desire to create educational and social opportunities for the children of interfaith families. Some focus primarily on celebrating holidays and life-cycle events together; others have regular monthly meetings with discussions on a broad array of topics.

New and emerging interfaith groups can learn from the experiences of others. According to Jaida n'ha Sandra, an expert on salons (groups of people who regularly gather in living rooms or coffee shops to discuss a variety of topics, in the process forming a community), a new group must be initiated by someone. "It might be one person who has decided on his or her own . . ., it might be a core group of three to six organizers, or it might be 15 or 20 people drawn from a network of friends or a membership list who are working together to form the group. Whoever makes the initial decisions for a fledgling salon is bound to have a strong impact on its future leadership." Sandra suggests that the original organizer(s) should have: lots of energy, social savvy, a large circle of friends and acquaintances, and a big living room. Also helpful would be: passion about the issues facing interfaith families, an open mind, and flexibility.

If one person initiates the group, it is important for that person to allow the group to emerge and develop on its own, with leadership gradually being shared by many or all members. If the group's original organizer continues to control everything from meeting times to agendas to phone calls, she will find herself burned out, probably within a year. It is better to share responsibility gradually among members of a core group. Sandra describes how her own core group emerged: "We had a brainstorming session, split the leadership of future activities among us, built a phone tree to share the calling chores, opened up the [group] to other friends, and made donations to cover supplies." Be ready for a long and sometimes difficult process of reaching consensus—it can take several such meetings to hash out all the details to everyone's satisfaction. "The domineering people disagree heatedly, the reserved people don't get heard at all, factions develop, or compromises that don't satisfy anybody are reached. No one is to blame: few of us have been trained in facilitating group process. On the other hand, if [groups] that start with this kind of whole-group communication can get through the beginning negotiations, they are less likely to run out of steam in the future. If they can survive their rocky start, they have proven their intention to continue dealing with the problems and joys of being together."[1]

In the following pages, profiles of several established interfaith couples' groups will help shed light on the various goals and methods used.[2]

The Chicago Jewish-Catholic Couples' Dialogue Group

Dan and Abbe Josephs are two of the founders and coordinators of the Chicago Jewish-Catholic Couples' Dialogue Group. Dan, who is Catholic, is an attorney practicing in Illinois. Abbe, who is Jewish, is a computer engineer. When they decided to get married, they found a sympathetic priest who in turn helped them find a rabbi to co-officiate at their ceremony. Several years after their wedding, they asked the priest if there existed a support group they could join. The priest, who had just met another interfaith couple, didn't know of any existing group but suggested that they start one. The first meeting drew ten couples in 1988 and met in a church rectory. Soon the group found a rabbi who was willing to serve along with the Catholic clergy in a supportive capacity. In 1998, the group has grown to a mailing list of 500 couples ranging from couples who are dating to those who have been married over 25 years. It has monthly meetings, as well as special seasonal celebrations and quarterly workshops on how to plan an interfaith wedding (attendence at this last is required of interfaith couples as part of premarital counseling by some local clergy). A family religious school for children is in its fifth year, and the group has recently started a small group for young married couples with children.

Based on a decade of experiences, the Josephses offer advice on how to start a local group. "There are many ways to find couples. One approach is to talk to the clergy at your church and/or temple. Contact other churches and synagogues in your area. Try advertising in the local paper and in church and temple bulletins—people who see these advertisements may refer interfaith couples to you."

The Chicago group relies on the guidance and support of its affiliated clergypeople, both Christian and Jewish. "Our clergy have helped us to be authentic to our faiths. It may also be easier for you to gain the support of clergy if your group does not adulterate your respective religious beliefs and traditions. Our group does not try to create a new religion or blend and dilute Christianity or Judaism."

The New Haven, Connecticut Group

Christina Giebisch-Mohrer, an artist living in New Haven, Connecticut, with her two daughters and her husband Peter, founded a small independent group for interfaith families in her living room in 1990. She had been involved with an outreach program run by the New Haven Jewish Community Center. Though its programs were informative, "they left me dissatisfied. I wanted a group in which families worked together to find meaningful ways of integrating two religious traditions, one that valued each couple's search to express, practice, and teach their children what they believed was essential to their understanding of themselves as Jews and Christians. Such a group did not exist in New Haven."

So Giebisch-Mohrer created one. She invited a handful of interfaith couples to get together and discuss their specific needs and desires. Initially the focus of their meetings was on the struggle for self-definition. Everyone wanted to understand better what their own faith meant to them and to their spouses.

After several months, when they felt cohesive as a group, they invited a Christian clergyperson and a learned Jew to help deepen their discussions. The role of these two women in the group was fluid. Initially they served primarily as teachers—helping group members understand baffling concepts, difficult religious language, and poorly understood historical contexts. With time they came more and more to speak from their own experiences.

Giebisch-Mohrer remembers that "it was a priority for us to create an interfaith community with which our children could identify. We did this by coming together to celebrate holidays as whole families, as well as by gathering for fun social occasions. Both kinds of events helped our children to get to know one another and to realize that they were not alone in being part of an interfaith family."

During the first year Giebisch-Mohrer and her husband ran the meetings. They always got input from the group, but the actual agenda was in their hands. As the group became more established, they changed this format. The whole group now has one large planning session every six months, when they agree on topics and activities, choose dates, and have each family volunteer to facilitate one meeting. The group meets regularly in the fellowship room of a Congregational church. Twice a year they do gardening work on its grounds to thank the church for use of the space.

Discussion topics have included the High Holidays, with a focus on forgiveness from a Jewish and a Christian perspective; Christmas, Hanukkah, and the creation of family rituals; the meaning and experience of Passover, Easter, and Communion; baptism, bris, and naming ceremonies; Jewish and Christian views of death and the afterlife; and the meaning and practice of the Sabbath. The group has also had holiday celebrations with their children for Hanukkah, Christmas, and Passover. During the summer they gather for a potluck on the beach.

Because they are aware that integrating too many new people at one time could jeopardize the intimacy the group has achieved, group members have been careful about maintaining the size of the group, and not letting it grow too quickly.

As group members have learned about their faiths and have satisfied to some degree their need for adult discussion, the group's focus has turned to the children. They began a Sunday School program, now in its fourth year. It meets bimonthly and uses a curriculum created by a group member herself—focusing alternately on Jewish and Christian holidays and themes. Last year the oldest pupil turned 13 and wrote his own "affirmations" ceremony.

Giebisch-Mohrer is conscious of how the group has evolved over time. Citing the group's current emphasis on religious education for its children, she sees that "our group has fulfilled its original mission: to create a supportive environment for interfaith couples to explore their heritages safely and to grapple with how to raise their children. All of us have grown individually and collectively as a result of having been members of our interfaith group."

The Interfaith Families Project of Greater Washington DC

In 1995, four local women realized their common situation as mothers in interfaith families, and began to meet over coffee to conceptualize the Interfaith Families Project of Greater Washington, DC (IFFP). These four women, all partners in Jewish/Christian interfaith marriages, made a commitment to establish a community where interfaith families could celebrate their differences and learn from each other. What began as a small group has blossomed into a nurturing community of over 40 families.

Randi Field, a writer and former attorney, lives with her family in Silver Spring, Maryland, where she serves on the Board of IFFP. She reflects on how the group developed. "A central driving force for IFFP was the goal of creating an interfaith Sunday school. We wanted to share our historical and cultural heritages with our children and give them a place to belong with other children of interfaith families.

"In its first year, IFFP had one Sunday school for all the children. Last year, IFFP doubled in size and had two Sunday school classes, one for the younger children and one for the older children. IFFP has continued to grow, and this year we will have three Sunday school classes—a first/second grade class, a third/fourth grade class, and a fifth/sixth/seventh grade class. All classes will be staffed by experienced religious educators who will teach Judaism and Christianity from a historical perspective, as well as the various holidays and how they are celebrated.

"Another goal of the Sunday school is to teach the children that it is truly better to give than to receive. To that end, the Sunday school curriculum will be tied to our community service program. This past year, IFFP families donated Christmas presents to refugee children and Easter baskets to families with HIV-AIDS. At a shelter for homeless women, we turned an arid patch of land into a colorful garden. At a shelter for women and children, we painted and spruced up rooms. We also did yard cleanup for elderly people who need assistance to live independently."

A new area for IFFP families has been the development of an adult education group. When a number of parents met while the children were in Sunday school, they discovered their own thirst for spiritual growth. They began to invite speakers to come and address the adults while the children were in class.

IFFP comes together on a number of occasions during the year. A December holiday potluck party, a well-attended Passover seder, and a coming-of-age ceremony for one family's daughter have been highlights of the group's communal activities.

An Interfaith Group in California's Bay Area

Members of "The Interfaith Community" come from all over the Peninsula of the San Francisco Bay Area. Their guiding spirit is the verse from Isaiah 56, "My house shall be called a house of prayer for all peoples." They are led by a local rabbi and priest. For the last nine years, the two clergy have also worked as a team, co-officiating at an average of 25 interfaith wedding ceremonies a year.

The Interfaith Community started under Rabbi Charles Familant's leadership in 1988. He wanted to do some teaching on Judaism, geared toward the interfaith couples he was marrying. "He's very good at creating respectful, tolerant space," says community member Alicia Torre. "He doesn't sit in judgment." Initially, Father John Hester was invited as an occasional speaker; he began to co-lead the group when the two clerics realized that participants in the growing community wanted equal coverage of both faiths.

According to its Statement of Purpose, the Interfaith Community is committed to developing "innovative forms of celebration" where "the different traditions may be celebrated together in a harmonious and mutually fulfilling fashion." The community's thoughtful and innovative holiday celebrations draw a crowd of interfaith families, their parents and their children. For such celebrations, the community has developed its own High Holiday prayerbooks and a seder service for the second night of Passover. At one December event, the group joined in singing Hanukkah songs and Christmas carols, and in lighting an Advent wreath and a menorah. The symbolism escaped no one when a candle in the menorah went out and was re-lit by one from the Advent wreath.

The community's gatherings begin with songs, blessings over wine and bread, and the lighting of Shabbat candles. Oscar Rosenbloom, whose family's Jewish musical tradition dates back to his great-grandfather, serves as the community's cantor. "You're not going to make religious institutions change to allow interfaith couples to feel as comfortable as they do in an interfaith community," says Rosenbloom. "We try to empower such couples to recognize that they stand between the institutional cracks, and we welcome them to join us."

The Interfaith Community, which has a mailing list of a hundred couples, holds discussion meetings on the third Friday evening of the month, in the rectory of a local church. Sometimes the discussion meetings include a potluck dinner and guest speakers from both Christian and Jewish traditions. Past and future discussion topics include: women in congregations; the Vatican's attitude toward Judaism and the Jewish people; rites of passage in Judaism and Christianity; and parents of interfaith couples.

The group publishes a community newsletter with a monthly calendar, enabling members to pick and choose which events to attend. "We are trying to build a flexible community that will endure and serve many needs," says Torre. "Many of our members are alienated from religious institutions. Many are simply looking for a way to celebrate with a group of interfaith couples."

As Torre mentioned, there has been strong emotion against "institutionalizing" the community, as represented by forming a board or paying dues. Programs are financed by voluntary individual contributions, and community members pay an annual fee of $20 to receive the newsletter. Members agree that a large part of the community's strength is its spontaneity and flexibility.

The community grows continually, as couples newly married by the priest-rabbi team filter in. "There are enough things going on," says Torre, "that meetings remain small." As with other similar groups, the Interfaith Community works hard to strike a comfortable balance between inclusiveness and intimacy.

In addition to the groups profiled here, there are perhaps a dozen other independent local interfaith groups existing or in formation around the country. Besides these independent groups, there are hundreds of local outreach programs sponsored by Jewish groups. For some interfaith families, especially if they are leaning toward the decision to create a Jewish home, workshops and support groups sponsored by their local temple or Jewish community center are a good way to begin to delve into the questions they face.

Support Groups in the Jewish Community

As the Jewish community looks for ways to respond to the soaring national intermarriage rate, outreach programs for interfaith families are growing in number and importance. Congregation Emanuel, a Reform temple in Denver and a national leader in Jewish outreach to interfaith couples and families, has pioneered an educational program for unaffiliated children of interfaith couples. Called "Stepping Stones—To a Jewish Me," the two-year afternoon Sunday school builds Jewish identity and self-esteem, with emphases on experiential learning and respect for other religions. Open to children from ages 5 to 18, Stepping Stones provides basic knowledge of Judaism, including holidays, traditions, history, life cycle events, and religious symbols, all in a relaxed environment independent from the temple's religious school. At the beginning of each unit, parents receive an explanatory letter and guide to the material that their children will be studying. There are educational events for the whole family. During the program's second year, there is an optional "parent track," enabling parents to share in the educational, cultural, and religious aspects of the program, and providing tools for the non-Jewish partner's understanding of Judaism.

Children and parents are encouraged to talk about themselves and their families, so that they realize others have similar family situations. A 1991 study found that 89% of the parents involved in Stepping Stones felt that their heritage was respected. About 50% of the families who have participated in Stepping Stones since its beginning have either joined congregations, attend Jewish schools, or have entered the Jewish community in some way.

In the words of Saundra Heller, the developer of Stepping Stones, the program "is the beginning of a process. The families represent every need and position on the spectrum. Stepping Stones endeavors to provide the tools to encourage a family to choose one religion. Many Stepping Stones children and families move into Jewish education and involvement. Their journey is beginning, not ending."

Since it began at Emanuel in 1985, the program has spread to temples from Florida to California to New York. If you have not affiliated with a synagogue but want your children to identify with the Jewish part of their heritage, look for a Stepping Stones program at a synagogue in your area.[3]

For interfaith families considering Judaism as the family faith, another good program is Pathways, run by the United Jewish Federation of MetroWest New Jersey. Pathways is designed for families who think they might want to affiliate with a Jewish congregation, but who need additional information and education about Judaism before making the decision.

Pathways is modeled after the Stepping Stones program. Its literature describes the Pathways program's goal: "To provide knowledge of the basic elements of Jewish life, traditions and history while remaining completely compatible with contemporary secular society. Participating children, and their parents, will experience a non-pressured view into Judaism's vast cultural heritage."

The program, which began in January of 1991, is open to children between the ages of 5 and 18 whose parents desire to give them an opportunity to learn more about their Jewish heritage. There is no tuition fee, and a family can participate in the program for a maximum of two years. Parents "who recognize the need for positive Jewish identification for their children" are asked to share in the social, educational and cultural aspects of the Pathways program. Program literature assures parents that the program teachers "are particularly aware of the special needs of young people whose parents come from different religious and cultural backgrounds."

Over a one-year period, Pathways classes provide an introduction to the various elements of basic Judaism such as holidays, history, life cycle events, Jewish culture, religious symbols and practice lived through the literature, art and language of Jewish people. The curriculum includes an emphasis on understanding and respect for other religions "according to the needs, interests and sensitivity of the students and their families."

As part of the curriculum, children and parents participate in separate educational classes. Families come together for such joint events as a model Seder, model Shabbat celebrations, decoration of a *sukkah* (outdoor booth built for the harvest holiday Sukkot), and *tzedakah* (charity) programs. Families who choose to re-enroll for a second year of the program go through the same general curriculum, but with different activities and specific lessons based on the same cycle of holidays. "This second year serves to reinforce what families learned in the first year," reports Lynne Wolfe, the program's director.

The Pathways program does not try to hide its ultimate goal—"the transition of these families into synagogue membership, the children into religious school, and the opting for Judaism as the family's religion." The teachers and administrators of the program work toward this goal with refreshing sensitivity and open-mindedness. Wolfe is enthusiastic about what Pathways is achieving. "We are reawakening the Jewish partners' faith, sparking their interest in learning, teaching the children and providing them with knowledge and a sense of belonging. All this in a non-threatening, comfortable atmosphere!"

Families who have graduated from the Pathways program seem unabashedly excited about their experience. "Prior to coming to the Pathways program I was estranged from my Jewish roots," writes one parent. "The program provided us with a safe and inviting atmosphere for both my husband and myself to explore our thoughts and feelings about religion and relationships. While I was busy working on my own identity, my daughter's identity began to emerge. The program has helped me to gather the strength to challenge my fears and beliefs and allow Judaism to be part of our lives."

Another graduating parent writes, "I can't say that Pathways has provided all the answers to what is a complicated and difficult situation, but it has helped to add to our family life a religious aspect and spirituality that I believe we needed." One parent stressed the communal aspect of the program: "Pathways has given our two children an opportunity to be with other children from interfaith families. It has allowed them to feel a part of a group instead of somehow different from their peers."

According to Ms. Wolfe, the program serves between twelve and 28 families each year. She finds that about half of the families who graduate from the Pathways program go on to join synagogues. Ms. Wolfe is a strong advocate on behalf of these families, often calling the rabbi of a local temple to smooth the way before a family's first visit. When asked, she accompanies families to family services or special programs at the temple they are considering, "to help ease the transition." Ms. Wolfe also makes a point of calling every family who has graduated from the Pathways program at least once a year, to check on their status, offer encouragement, and provide additional information. In this way, even if a family has not made the decision to affiliate with a local synagogue, they still have a connection to the local Jewish community.[4]

Therapy: Another Option for Help and Support

Like their same-faith counterparts, Jewish/Christian couples face instances of disagreement and discord in their lives together. As they search for help in resolving these differences, not every interfaith couple will be ready or willing to dive into a group situation, whether it be an independent interfaith families group or a temple-sponsored group. Some may prefer the more intimate and individually focused atmosphere of family therapy.

This section looks at the questions raised when interfaith couples consider professional therapy. Does the fact that such couples come from two different religious backgrounds make their inevitable disagreements more frequent or profound? And is there any correlation between their religious and cultural differences and the ability of a therapist to help them through the particularly difficult times?

This section includes articles by professionals with extensive experience counseling Jewish/Christian couples. The authors, while placing different emphases on theory and method, come to a number of common conclusions. All agree that, to benefit from therapy, both partners in an interfaith relationship must examine their religious and cultural identities and carefully define and communicate their individual and common priorities. All suggest that the strongest catalyst for potential discord is the arrival of children on the scene. And all agree that an interfaith couple, like any other, can survive difficult discord, provided both partners are committed to the relationship.

When the partners in a Jewish/Christian marriage decide to seek professional help, they may have difficulty finding a therapist willing to consider their special needs. Joan Rachel Goldberg, editor of *Family Therapy News*, contends that most marriage and family therapists are ignorant of the effects spirituality has on couples. She writes that "Talk of the soul may confuse or scare some therapists. . . . They are content to relegate religion and spirituality to the realm of the unmeasurable and unscientific, subjects best left ignored." A helpful therapist, while not needing specific experience with interfaith couples, will have certain characteristics, including a willingness to discuss religious and spiritual issues.

In their classic resource, **Ethnicity and Family Therapy**, Monica McGoldrick, John Pearce and Joseph Giordano explore the issue of intermarriage from a psychotherapist's perspective. They find that "Couples who choose to [inter]marry are usually seeking a rebalance of the characteristics of their own ethnic background. They are moving away from some values as well as toward others."

The authors have found that stress increases an interfaith couple's difficulties. "Typically, we tolerate differences when we are not under stress. In fact, we find them appealing. However, when stress is added to a system, our tolerance for difference diminishes. We become frustrated if we are not understood in ways that fit with our wishes and expectations. . . . In our experience, much of therapy involves helping family members recognize each other's behavior as a reaction from a different frame of reference."

How Can Therapy Help Interfaith Couples?

Marilyn B. Robie, Ph.D., and Arthur L. Shechet, Ph.D., are partners in an interfaith marriage and practice clinical psychology in Lexington, Kentucky. They have two children. Robie and Schechet suggest that conflict in marriage is actually positive, and that learning to resolve conflict is essential to maintaining the long-term health of the relationship. They have observed that for interfaith couples, issues related to religious values, beliefs, and practices will be faced at different stages in the relationship. "In the period leading to the marriage, the couple is often focused on dealing with the impact of the relationship on their own families. Often religious differences between the partners are minimized in order to solidify the relationship and to present a unified stance to the families. In the early stages of marriage prior to the arrival of children, differences are often harmonized and smoothed, perhaps even celebrated, as the partners revel in the novelty of their union and the excitement of discovered differences.

"The inevitable fault line for interfaith couples is the arrival of children. Not all couples engage in serious negotiations concerning issues of faith and practice prior to this point. Whether a prior agreement has been developed or not, many people experience the issue with much more intensity of feeling when there is a child. This intensity is often unanticipated; discussions of religious identity and practice when there are children involved may be very different in emotional tone than those that occurred prior to children. As is true for many issues that arise in a marriage, differences that were a source of attraction, excitement, and interest early in a relationship can become points of friction later. Sometimes underlying serious problems in a marriage can congeal around a particular issue, such as religious affiliation, and infuse it with much more hostility than would seem warranted.

"An interfaith couple can have a framework for issues of religious faith that basically works for their family and still have to negotiate some of the particulars throughout the course of their marriage. These disagreements are not necessarily signs that there are major problems that require professional intervention. The capacity to have conflicts and resolve them is very important in an enduring relationship. However, when disagreements do not get resolved, when they become perpetual sources of divisiveness and not just difference in a marriage, they can contribute to the long-standing resentments and mutual alienation that are ruinous for a relationship and destructive to all members of the family.

"There may be telltale signs that such a process is occurring, as when spouses begin to avoid talking about important concerns. Increased emotional and physical distance can signal that there are barriers that are becoming more difficult to overcome. At times, increased marital distance is accompanied by heightened involvement on the part of one or both partners with the children in the family.

Couples in trouble sometimes begin isolating themselves more from their friends and community, although some distressed couples cope with their difficulties by becoming overinvolved with other activities so as to minimize time alone and together. Extended families may be allowed to intrude and create friction in a persistent way, and the couple ends up arguing about those matters, masking the more significant problems between spouses. For interfaith couples, a primary problem is an inability to come to a unified stance about issues of religious affiliation and practice. A unified stance in this situation does not mean that husband and wife are the same, but rather that they have developed a truly agreed upon solution for dealing with their differences."

When a couple has determined that they need to gain some additional perspective on their relationship and problems, Robie and Schechet suggest that it consider professional marital therapy. "Therapy for couples is an option to be explored before a problem becomes so divisive that divorce is considered an option. Therapy is much more effective in the context of a relationship where there is a modicum of affection and commitment rather than in a 'last straw' scenario."

Robie and Schechet suggest that the couple seek out a therapist who is recommended by multiple sources, licensed by a professional regulatory board, and open to a phone or face-to-face interview prior to initiating treatment.

They believe that a competent therapist does not need to have extensive experience in dealing with interfaith couples in order to be effective. "For many couples, the interfaith issues may reflect problems with basic marital processes, such as effective communication, tolerating differing needs, and negotiating power and control. A good therapist will focus on developing new and healthier patterns between partners, rather than being the authoritative source of solutions for specific issues."

Dr. Irwin H. Fishbein, a rabbi and licensed marriage and family therapist, is director of the Rabbinic Center for Research and Counseling in Westfield, New Jersey. He has specialized in counseling interfaith couples for over 25 years, and firmly believes that professional help from a pastoral psychotherapist can provide an objective arena in which to explore emotionally charged issues that seem to defy any kind of resolution.

Fishbein has observed that one of the most common concerns expressed by intermarrying couples is how to deal with the religious identification of their children. "When discussing this," he reflects, "it is important that each mate begin by identifying and sharing feelings. It is vital to be able to listen to the other's feelings and to respond to them. Can you find some common thread that both of you can embrace? For instance, you may be able to agree that the most important part of a particular holiday celebration as you were growing up was family closeness and that it is this feeling that you want to preserve and give to your children."

Fishbein suggests that couples, whether or not they are currently in therapy, "always keep in mind that most of what is precious to each of you is a basic human want and usually not rooted in any particular religious tradition." He posits that the litmus test for understanding how well a problem has been solved is the level of comfort each mate experiences with the solution. "If you both do not feel good about a decision you have made, it is probably not a helpful decision for your relationship and it will need further exploration. Pursue the matter until you come to a better resolution."

Another professional who deals extensively with therapy and interfaith marriage, Esther Perel, M.A., is a couples and family therapist in New York. In Perel's experience, many conflicts that bring interfaith couples into therapy are explicitly related to their different cultural and religious backgrounds. "Among the issues most often presented are those concerning life-cycle transitions, relations with their families of origin, religious practice, celebration of holidays, and childrearing. Often couples seek help when they have reached a transition point in their relationship and/or are faced with the need to make a major commitment. Other concerns emerge periodically, corresponding to the religious calendar."

Sometimes couples, says Perel, focus exclusively on a "church-synagogue dichotomy, a Christmas-Hanukkah split, a me-you battle. When couples become thus polarized around their differences, the intensity and reactivity generated prevent them from dealing with any other issue in the relationship. They remain stuck around the all-consuming preoccupation of religious difference."

In this situation, each partner expends great amounts of energy trying to convince the other to change his or her beliefs and opinions. Perel notes that "To create change in an entangled situation, it is necessary to shift the focus from changing the other to defining oneself. This can be achieved by engaging in a guided exploration of each partner's identity and helping them articulate this to their partner. When each partner becomes more secure in him- or herself, the other becomes less threatening. With this reduction in anxiety, the partners can become creative in their negotiation of the cultural fabric of their family and the future identity of their children.

"Children often represent a blank screen against which the partners can project their ethnic and religious differences that they are loath to confront within themselves. Because children symbolize the continuity of the family, its values, and traditions, they bring into focus the differences of the partners' backgrounds—the challenge of transforming two cultures into one."[5]

Edwin H. Friedman, a rabbi and family therapist, has counseled thousands of interfaith couples and is well-known for his paper "The Myth of the Shiksa," which examines the interaction of culture and family dynamic when a family member decides to intermarry. He has found that effective therapy for families undergoing intermarriage focuses on the family processes rather than on the ideological issues. By helping family members to understand the way the family works, he diverts attention and emotion away from the divisive idea. He suggests that the basis of the myth is "one generally misunderstood notion about the relationship of culture and family process. Once that relationship is understood to be almost the reverse of what is often assumed, new perceptions become available for understanding all families, as well as for creating strategies for therapeutic change."

Divorce in Interfaith Families

Divorce is certainly not a topic that most Jewish/Christian families want to think about, but, just as it happens for same-faith couples, it happens to many interfaith couples. The phenomenon of divorce among interfaith families has been studied and analyzed, with mixed results. One 1987 study by Rabbi Allen S. Maller, of Temple Akiba in Culver City, California, found that the divorce rate for Jewish/Christian couples is 133 percent higher than for Jewish couples (who, by most accounts, have a lower than average divorce rate).

According to Joseph Guttman, university professor and author of **Divorce in Psychosocial Perspective**, who has studied the studies, "the divorce rate in interfaith marriages has consistently revealed itself to be higher than in religiously homogamous marriages. . . . Furthermore, when one of the partners in the marriage has no religious affiliation and the other does, the probability of divorce also increases." However, Guttman explains that some of the higher incidence of divorce among intermarried couples may be due to other factors such as age at marriage and social class differences. "Some of the effect," he goes on to say, "may be due to there being more points of conflict over children's socialization and differences in values, traditions, and relevant habits and practices." Furthermore, Guttman cites a 1989 study which found no effect of religion on the divorce rate. Obviously, the research done to date on divorce among intermarried couples is not conclusive.

Divorce and Children's Religious Identity

Despite how difficult it is for a happily intermarried couple to consider the possibility of divorce, parents should plan consciously in advance for the religious education of their children in the event of divorce, even if they don't anticipate facing this legal issue down the road. In the United States we have a federal legal system under which matters of divorce are governed by state law. Consequently, there is no unified legal precedent or doctrine in these areas, but rather a range of possibilities for outcome based on various state laws. It is very important, given this legal range of outcomes, for interfaith couples to consider these issues in advance, so that their decisions about the religious upbringing of their children can be carried out even if the family splits or changes.

Children whose family structure is being changed may rely in a simple way on their religion as a support to guide them through the changes. Parents need to think long and hard about what they teach their children, and about how what they teach will affect their children's ability to cope with difficult situations.

When interfaith couples disagree over religious training, their children almost always get caught in the middle. So it is essential for Jewish/Christian parents in the process of divorce to present a united front and avoid feelings of religious competition, which could be internalized by already vulnerable children.

When Olivia Mellon Shapiro, a Jewish woman from Brooklyn, divorced her Indian Hindu husband, they had a one-and-a-half-year-old son. The couple sought therapy and mediation to help them through the split. Shapiro believes that their flexibility and affection for one another have been the key to an amicable interfaith divorce. "We wrote into our divorce agreement that if things got strained between us and if one of us saw the need, we could ask the other to return to our therapist to work out our differences. We have done that three times, for one session each, in the eleven years since our divorce. Each time, it has helped us proceed harmoniously for the next three or four years. This may sound amazingly clear and easy, but the fact is, we were always good friends— even before our marriage—and we are committed to keeping our communication and our relationship clear and positive, for the sake of our son and to honor our friendship."

What Happens to Children When Interfaith Couples Break Up?

Rabbi Dr. Arthur Blecher is both an ordained rabbi and a psychotherapist in private practice in Washington, DC. The majority of couples he sees in his counseling practice are interfaith couples. His clinical experience shows that "when interfaith parents separate, the support system they have built for their children's religious identity falls apart far more extensively than for same-faith couples. Ironically, interfaith parents who have elected to raise their children with one specific religious identity, which is the approach that receives the greatest support and approval from the religious establishment, find this to be especially problematic if they break up."

Blecher finds that in many cases a parent must undertake the responsibility for providing a religious upbringing different from that parent's own religious identity. The situation becomes exacerbated when a parent forms a new relationship, and the child of the interfaith separation is blended into the new family. "In my practice I have come across families where, for example, a Christian couple with Christian children are also raising a Jewish child from a previous relationship. I once testified as an expert witness in a very painful custody case where this was the central issue. Interfaith parents, whether or not they are considering divorce, should work hard to build a solid support system for their children's religious identity, a system that can withstand the trials of family change."

Rebecca Korzec, a professor at the University of Baltimore School of Law, has written on the growing phenomenon of religious differences between divorced parents.[6] This phenomenon, she asserts, forces the courts to face some tough questions. "What role should the religious beliefs and needs of parents and children play in child custody and visitation decisions? Should courts even consider religious preferences or should they remain 'neutral' by refusing to consider religious questions under any circumstances?"

Korzec points to the case of an interfaith family in Colorado. Mr. Simms was Jewish; his wife-to-be was Catholic. They married in a Jewish religious ceremony and raised their children as Jews. Following their separation, Mrs. Simms resumed the practice of Catholicism, taking the children to church with her. Mr. Simms objected. In 1987, a Colorado district court granted physical custody of the Simms children to their Catholic mother, while granting "spiritual custody" "for the purposes of determing religious training" to their Jewish father.

Says Korzec: "Because only a few states dictate the factors to be weighed in determining the child's best interests, courts have wide discretion in considering religious differences between parents. Some courts apply a joint or shared custody approach to the religion question." This is what happened in the Simms case in Colorado. "By 1988," says Korzec, "more than thirty states had enacted legislation permitting, encouraging, or even compelling joint custody arrangements in which both divorced parents decide major issues concerning the child. In some instances, the child even divides time equally between both parental homes."

Korzec suggests that the initial enthusiasm expressed by the legal system regarding joint custody arrangements has waned recently, as courts have realized the difficulty inherent in forcing divorced partners to cooperate on issues such as the religious education of their children. She writes that "Individuals experiencing the trauma and disorientation of divorce often seek solace in their ethnic and religious roots. Joint custody is simply inappropriate under these circumstances."

A Pennsylvania case, *Zummo v. Zummo*, shows the difficulties inherent in the current judicial approach to religion in custody disputes. Paula and David Zummo were married in 1978, had three children, and divorced in 1988. Paula was raised as a Jew and "actively practiced her faith since childhood." The trial court concluded that the parties had discussed their religious differences prior to their marriage and had agreed orally that any children would be raised in the Jewish faith.

Following their separation, the Zummos agreed to share legal custody. Paula had primary physical custody, subject to the father's partial physical custody on alternating weekends and certain holidays and vacation periods. But David refused to have the children attend Jewish Sunday school during his visitation, taking them to Roman Catholic services instead.

The trial court held that Mr. Zummo was obliged to arrange for the children's attendance at Jewish Sunday school, and that he would not be permitted to take the children to religious services contrary to the Jewish faith. The Pennsylvania Superior Court reversed, concluding that "it is constitutionally impermissible to decide a custody or visitation dispute, in whole or in part, on the basis of a determination of or consideration of the parent's relative devoutness."

Korzec suggests that "Zummo exemplifies the shortcoming of the current judicial approach, in that it fails to promote post-divorce family stability by ignoring the legitimate and reasonable religious contracts formed by the pre-divorce family. Simply stated, the Zummo pre-divorce contract reflected the parties' intent to be a Jewish family. Before their divorce, the Zummos chose to raise their children in one religion, rather than two. Their agreement should not have been breached merely because the parents divorced."

In the Zummo case, the court failed to consider the effect of the ruling on the Zummo children. In Korzec's words, "The tragedy of Zummo is that it completely frustrates reasonable family expectations and stability at precisely the moment they are most critical." She suggests that parents in interfaith families create contracts that would bind them to their original decisions regarding religious education for their children in the event of divorce. The courts' ability to enforce such contracts, she posits, "would increase the possibility for stability and certainty for both parents and children."

Mediation as an Option in Interfaith Divorce

Not all interfaith families going through divorce choose to address their disagreements in the legal system. A growing number of families are turning to mediation as a gentler, less antagonistic alternative to divorce court. Doris T. Friedman, P.C., has worked as an attorney for 37 years and has been involved in private mediation for 15 years. She is the founder and past president of the New York Council on Divorce Mediation, and is a practicing member of the Academy of Family Mediators.

Friedman notes that "Any family that anticipates a separation or divorce is faced with countless problems and hurdles to overcome—custody, visitation, extended family relations, support, equitable distribution and lifestyles. For the interfaith family, all of these problems are compounded by questions of religion. When divorce leads to physical relocation, children who are already heartbroken and confused may be further stressed by communities who do not accept their unique backgrounds."

Friedman describes mediation as "a process whereby the parties sit together (or in separate rooms) at the same time with a neutral professional who is able to assist the parties in resolving their own differences, rather than accepting mandated resolutions from a court. Mediation can diminish the sharpness and adversarial nature of separation, and couples who select mediation as the method of resolving their disputes are already one step ahead of those who have chosen the adversarial legal arena. For parents who must learn to co-parent whether or not they are separated, mediation is both a method of resolution and of education, as parents learn to communicate with each other in a different relationship. Parents must learn to interact with sensitivity, patience, and commitment to the hard work of resolution. When the mediation process works well, interfaith children can grow up to be comfortable in both of their worlds, with pride in both heritages and solid in their knowledge that they are loved enough to prevail over their parents' anger and hostility toward each other."

Friedman is quick to point out that choosing mediation over legal action does not erase the pain of divorce. "But what people who are willing to enter the alternative dispute resolution process have learned is the ability to bridge, in the true sense of the word, the differences all families have. Decisions reached through mediation come from the individuals themselves, and thus have more meaning to the parties involved."

For interfaith families in the Chicago area, there is now a program designed specifically to help them get through the emotional anguish of deciding religious upbringing for children of divorce, without dragging the decision through divorce courts. The Interfaith Family Mediation Project is co-directed by Professor Katheryn M. Dutenhaver and the Reverend Craig B. Mousin, both of the DePaul University College of Law, in Chicago, Illinois.

Say Mousin and Dutenhaver: "Families have often avoided this religious decision, even when the marriage was not threatened with divorce. Parents may never have fully articulated their own religious beliefs or never fully developed their own faith. In the worst of cases, parents may use control over the religious upbringing of children as a means for negotiating other benefits from the other spouse." And, after re-examining their own beliefs, divorcing parents often re-commit themselves to their religion, leaving little ground for negotiation about the children.

The question of a child's religious custody is further complicated by the fact that many children of divorced parents spend the week with the parent who has custody, and the weekend—when many religious observances occur—with the other parent. And often there is pressure from both extended families to rear the children in their own faith.

The Interfaith Family Mediation Project, believed to be the first of its kind, was begun in March 1991. According to Rev. Mousin, the project tries "to enable the families to work together to minimize the difficult consequences of the breakup." The project is voluntary and designed to help families make a tough religious decision without judicial intervention. Voluntary agreement enhances the likelihood of compliance and fosters the best interests of the children and the parents. The voluntary participation of parents may also remove constitutional challenges to later divorce proceedings.

The project has three objectives: (1) to provide parents with a means to resolve the question of the religious upbringing of their children without the tension of a court-ordered solution; (2) to allow parents to participate in mediation with the help of clergy of their own faith; and (3) to free the courts from making decisions that are both outside of their normal decision-making process and perhaps improper under the First Amendment.

Mediation sessions are confidential and include the mediator, each parent, and a member of the clergy from each parent's faith. The parents each present their case in a mock courtroom at the law school over the course of two or three days. No lawyers are allowed to attend, and the couple is asked not to bring the children.

Dutenhaver, an associate professor of law and a professional mediator since 1982, plans and conducts training for volunteer clergy, acts as the mediator, and is available for consultation throughout the mediation process. "We look at where the two parents live, the availability of religious services and schools in their community, and how they can best achieve their goals regarding the religious life of their children by choosing one faith or the other," she says.

A typical agreement might give religious custody to one parent while encouraging the child to attend religious services with the other parent, participate in readings at home or visit with the other parent on religious holidays. If such an agreement is reached, it is presented to the court by the couple's lawyers as part of the divorce settlement. If the couple cannot reach an agreement through the mediation project, it goes to the court to decide.

Mousin, executive director of the DePaul University College of Law Center for Church/State Studies (which sponsors the mediation project), is also an ordained minister in the United Church of Christ and an associate minister at the Wellington Avenue UCC. "To date," says Mousin, "most of the parties that have participated have found the program beneficial." And, given rising intermarriage and divorce rates, programs such as the Interfaith Family Mediation Project can be expected to crop up around the country. Says one rabbi who has worked with the project: "Even a rabbi or priest may have to say there is more than one true path to God. If God is looking, he wants people to get to the top. Maybe he's not concerned about which path they take."[7]

All Things Considered

Despite the heated discussions and occasional fights, despite the unexpected "time bombs" that can accompany life-cycle events, despite the pressures and pulls of extended families and religious communities, life in an interfaith family can be rich with joy, excitement and growth. If you commit yourselves to open and honest discussion, expect hard work and compromise, laugh often, and remember to enjoy the fullness of the two traditions your family comprises, you'll be well on the way to a successful interfaith marriage.

Afterword

There is a developing sense of community among interfaith families around the country. As evidenced by the growth of local interfaith groups and attendance at interfaith events, Jewish/Christian families, no matter what their individual decisions regarding home life and religious education, are finding one another and sharing common experiences and support.

We hope that this book will contribute to the strengthening of interfaith families themselves and of the ties between families who find themselves on a common path. The mission of Dovetail Publishing is to gather and disseminate information of interest to Jewish/Christian families. Please write to us and share your experiences.

Dovetail Publishing, Inc.
P.O. Box 19945
Kalamazoo, MI 49019
e-mail: dovetail@mich.com

Recent Research on Interfaith Marriage

In the last seven years, a significant number of doctoral candidates in the fields of psychology and sociology have chosen to examine the issues facing interfaith parents and children. In addition to the work done by Juliet Whitcomb (see pages 82–83), the following research projects have sought to analyze and quantify the available data.

Children of Interfaith Marriage

Beth Grossman (Ph.D. 1990, Fairleigh Dickinson University)

Sixty high school juniors and seniors participated, divided into the following three groups, based on their answers to a series of inventories: children with Catholic parents, children with Jewish parents, and children with intermarried parents. Children from intermarried families scored significantly higher on measures of self-esteem, need for uniqueness, self-actualization than did children of same-faith families. Children of interfaith marriage did not adopt more of an intrinsic religious orientation than did children of same-faith families. Children of interfaith marriages were found to be less frequent participants in religious activities than children of same-faith marriages, but were not found to be less socially involved than children of same-faith marriages. Results were not consistent with concerns about the negative impact of interfaith marriage on children.

The Dynamics of Interfaith Marriage Involving Jews

Evan Nelson (Ph.D. 1991, University of North Carolina at Chapel Hill)

Over 300 subjects completed questionnaires; of these, 121 married couples—same-faith, conversionary, and interfaith—were retained for analysis. Interfaith couples had less interest in and practice of Judaism than same-faith and conversionary couples. Intermarried Jews increased their involvement with Judaism since having married, but not as substantially as same-faith Jews. Christians' average levels of involvement with their religions had not changed since marriage. Marital power appeared to be imbalanced, in that Jews asked for and received support from their spouses for Jewish practices but were less forthcoming in offering support for the practice of their Christian spouses' religions. Marital satisfaction among same-faith, conversionary and interfaith couples was not found to be signficantly different. Most couples were raising their children primarily Jewish. Jews reported this was because they desired to pass on the Jewish culture to their children, while Christians were more interested in exposing their children to a religion. Many couples started planning the religious upbringing of their children before marriage, but did not finish the plan until after having had children. The correlation between early planning and marital satisfaction was not significant.

A Comparison of Interfaith, Conversionary, and Same-Faith Couples from a Family-of-Origin Perspective
Abby L. Friedman (Ph.D. 1992, DePaul University)

Participants included 93 couples in conversionary Jewish marriages, interfaith marriages with a born Jew and a born Christian, and same-faith Jewish marriages. Participants independently completed a questionnaire. Assessment of the responses led to the following conclusions. Born-Jewish participants reported a closer and more satisfying relationship with their parents than the born-Christian participants. A pattern of decreasing religiosity across generations was found among born Jews in interfaith marriages. Born-Jewish subjects in interfaith marriages were less likely to transmit a Jewish identity to their children than born-Jewish subjects in conversionary and same-faith marriages. It was postulated that born-Jewish women and born-Christian men in conversionary marriages might experience the greatest isolation, as they have deviated the most from conventional expectations regarding men's and women's roles, as borne out by the finding that both of these groups experienced greater distance from their parents and families-of-origin.

Jewish-Christian Dual Heritage: The Subjective Experience of Ten College-Age Children of Intermarriage
Tamara Barbasch (Ph.D. 1993, University of Pennsylvania)

Ten college-age children of Jewish/Christian mixed marriages participated in a series of three unstructured and semi-structured interviews. Material from participant narratives was thematically analyzed and findings were categorized by social relationships and experiences, parental harmony and mutual respect, parental acceptance and encouragement to explore, exposure to both heritages, multi-cultural awareness and appreciation of diversity, social and psychological marginality, multi-part identity and identity confusion.

Manifestation of Loyalty by Family Members of Interfaith Marriage
Susan Silverman LaDuca (Ph.D. 1993, Temple University)

Twelve couples were interviewed using in-depth, conjoint interviews. The attempt was not to answer a specific hypothesis but to discover and describe how the interfaith partners in long-term marriages negotiated the major events of their lives together. All 24 participants considered the expectations of their families of origin regarding marriage and child-rearing. Religious conviction did not seem to play a part in the course of action each couple elected. Half of the participants had eloped, while the other half had religious ceremonies. The majority of the children of the participants were provided with formal religious training. The few couples who opted to forego religious training for their children did provide the children with knowledge of their cultural roots.

Effects of Interfaith and Same-Faith Marriages on Children
Cathy Magnus (B.A. 1995, Rider University, Lawrenceville, NJ)

Magnus's interest in religions blossomed during her college years, sparked by her own decision to convert to Judaism. Her study investigated the effects of interfaith vs. same-faith marriages to test the following three hypotheses:

- whether a child from one type of marriage was more likely to follow the religion of a particular parent;
- whether the child would more consistently choose the religion of the parent of the same gender; and
- whether the child would consistently choose the religion of the more religious parent.

Sixty-nine American college undergraduates participated in this study. The first hypothesis, that children would follow the religion of one parent, whether it was a same-faith or interfaith marriage, was not supported by the test results. Furthermore, in the questionnaires, it was found that many subjects who were raised by parents to be religious were practicing different religions on their own, or no religion at all.

The second hypothesis, that the child in an interfaith marriage would follow the religion of the parent who is the same gender, was not supported. It seems that students tend to make these choices for themselves independently of their parents very often.

The third hypothesis was supported, as test results showed that there is a significant relationship in interfaith families between the parent of the higher religiosity and the religion that the child chooses. In a significant number of cases, it was found that the child followed the religion of the parent who was more religious. Perhaps this is attributable to the fact that the parent who is more religious cared more to share the beliefs and practices with the child, so it impacted the child more.

Attitudes Toward Intermarriage
B'nai B'rith Women (now Jewish Women International, Spring 1990)

B'nai B'rith Women commissioned a survey of its 100,000 members on attitudes toward intermarriage. The survey tallied approximately 1325 questionnaires completed by Jewish women.

About 50 percent of the respondents are 60 years old or older; 63 percent have at least one child who is or has been married. In sharp contrast to older respondents, among those under 40 who are or have been married, only 67 percent married husbands who were Jewish by birth.

Of those respondents whose children are married, less than half said that their children married Jews by birth. According to the executive summary of the survey, "given the intermarriage trend among younger members of B'nai B'rith Women, and among the married children of members, it appears that within a decade or two intermarried members will be more typical in the organization than in-married members."

A little more than 8 out of 10 respondents said they would prefer to see a 35-year-old daughter marry a Christian rather than remain single. A little more than 6 out of 10 opted for interfaith marriage over remaining single when the choice concerned a son.

Only 14 percent said they would try to dissuade a 35-year-old single daughter or granddaughter from intermarrying. Thirty-five percent said they would try to dissuade a 35-year-old son or grandson.

Just about half the respondents said they would make an effort to have a Christian daughter-in-law convert to Judaism, but only a little more than a third say they would do that with a Christian son-in-law.

While respondents were split on the issue of whether they would make the effort to convince a Christian son- or daughter-in-law convert to Judaism, the overwhelming majority would like to see their grandchildren raised exclusively in the Jewish tradition—even when the mother of the child is not Jewish.

More than three-quarters of the respondents believe that their Christian sons- or daughters-in-law should be welcome to membership in a synagogue. Half would want Christian sons- or daughters-in-law welcome to serve on synagogue boards.

More than 80 percent would consider their own grandchildren Jewish even if the children's mother is not Jewish, tacitly accepting a "patrilineal" standard for Jewish identity. While the overwhelming majority (75–80 percent) would like to see their grandchildren raised Jewish, a large minority (30–40 percent) is willing to see their grandchildren be exposed equally to Jewish and Christian traditions.

An Investigation of Faith Formation in Children of Catholic-Jewish Parents

Eileen O'Farrell Smith, longitudinal study funded by the Lilly Endowment.

Smith is a Catholic full-time mom of three interfaith kids and project director of a study funded for three years by the Lilly Endowment through the Archdiocese of Chicago.

The study is monitoring and chronicling the faith formation and development of cultural identity in thirteen children of Catholic/Jewish parents, charting the evolution of the thought and decision-making processes of their parents as they create a faith system in their own families, and concluding whether these children's dual faith traditions will likely contribute to or detract from their religious identities as adults.

The faith function of these children is being monitored, charting those connections between their day-to-day existence and their spiritual lives and identifying factors which influence their faith development. Secondarily, the thought and decision-making processes of these ten sets of parents are being studied as they evolve and create a system of faith within their families, in the context of their individual histories.

In addition to being observed in the classroom twice a year, the children are each interviewed. They may respond orally, in writing, or by drawing. Each of their parents is asked for certain baseline data regarding that parent's religious history and past and present religious practices, ideologies, attitudes, hopes, and expectations. Parental willingness to accept certain established rituals and rites of passage for their children or to create their own within the context of their individual family's system of faith is assessed. Against this baseline data, the parents will be interviewed in order to monitor whether and whatever changes may occur in their decision-making processes.

Resources for Interfaith Families

Current Basic Books on Interfaith Marriage

Glaser, Gabrielle. **Strangers to the Tribe: Portraits of Interfaith Marriage.**
Boston: Houghton Mifflin Company, 1997.

Mayer, Egon. **Love and Tradition: Marriage Between Jews and Christians.**
New York: Schocken Books, 1987.

McClain, Ellen Jaffe. **Embracing the Stranger: Intermarriage and the
Future of the American Jewish Community.** New York: BasicBooks,
1995.

*Reuben, Steven Carr. **Making Interfaith Marriage Work.** Rocklin, CA:
Prima Publishing, 1994.

*Rosenbaum, Mary Heléne Pottker and Stanley Ned. **Celebrating Our
Differences: Living Two Faiths in One Marriage.** Shippensburg, PA:
Ragged Edge Press, 1994.

Schneider, Susan Weidman. **Intermarriage: The Challenge of Living with
Differences Between Christians & Jews.** New York: The Free Press,
1989.

Other Books on Interfaith Marriage

(These are out-of-print or hard to find, but worth looking for in your library
or used bookstore.)

Cowan, Paul and Rachel. **Mixed Blessings: Overcoming the Stumbling
Blocks in an Interfaith Marriage.** New York: Penguin Books, 1987.

*Petsonk, Judy, and Jim Remsen. **The Intermarriage Handbook: A Guide
for Jews and Christians.** New York: Quill/William Morrow, 1988.

Romain, Rabbi Jonathan A. **Till Faith Do Us Part: Couples Who Fall in
Love Across the Religious Divide.** London: Fount, 1996.

*Rosenberg, Rabbi Roy A., Father Peter Meehan, and Rev. John Wade Payne.
**Happily Intermarried: Authoritative Advice for a Joyous Jewish-
Christian Marriage.** New York: Collier Books, 1988.

Sandmel, Samuel. **When a Jew and Christian Marry.** Philadelphia:
Fortress, 1977.

Silver, Rabbi Samuel M. **Mixed Marriage Between Jew and Christian.**
New York: Arco Publishing, 1977.

Cultural and Religious Differences

*Crohn, Joel. **Mixed Matches: How to Create Successful Interracial, Interethnic, and Interfaith Marriages.** New York: Fawcett Columbine, 1995.

Engel, Edith S. and Henry W. **One God: Peoples of the Book.** New York: Pilgrim Press, 1990.

Firestone, Rabbi Tirzah. **With Roots in Heaven: One Woman's Passionate Journey into the Heart of Her Faith.** New York: Penguin Putnam, Inc., 1998.

Interreligious Council of San Diego. **Bridging Our Faiths.** New York/ Mahwah, NJ: Paulist Press, 1997.

Kohls, L. Robert. **Survival Kit for Overseas Living.** Intercultural Press, 1984.

Matlins, Stuart M. and Arthur J. Magida, **How to Be a Perfect Stranger: A Guide to Etiquette in Other People's Religious Ceremonies,** vols. 1 and 2. Woodstock, VT: Jewish Lights Publishing, 1996 and 1997.

McGoldrick, Monica, John K. Pearce, and Joseph Giordano. **Ethnicity and Family Therapy.** New York: Guilford Press, 1982.

Interfaith Parenting

*Berends, Polly Berrien. **Gently Lead, or How to Teach Your Children About God While Finding Out for Yourself.** New York: HarperCollins, 1991.

Brandt, Anthony. "Do Kids Need Religion?" **Parenting,** Dec. 1987.

Catalfo, Phil. "Paths to God." **Parenting,** March 1993, pp. 88–93.

Fay, Martha. **Do Children Need Religion? How Parents Today Are Thinking About the Big Questions.** New York: Pantheon Books, 1993.

*Fitzpatrick, Jean Grasso. **Something More: Nurturing Your Child's Spiritual Growth.** New York: Penguin Books, 1991.

*Goodman-Malamuth, Leslie, and Robin Margolis. **Between Two Worlds: Choices for Grown Children of Jewish-Christian Parents.** New York: Pocket Books, 1992.

*Gruzen, Lee F. **Raising Your Jewish/Christian Child: How Interfaith Parents Can Give Children the Best of Both Their Heritages.** New York: Newmarket Press, 1990.

Heller, David, Ph.D. **Talking to Your Child About God: A Book for Families of All Faiths.** New York: Bantam, 1988.

Hollander, Annette, M.D. **How to Help Your Child Have a Spiritual Life: A Parent's Guide to Inner Development.** New York: A & W Publishers, Inc., 1980.

King, Andrea. **If I'm Jewish and You're Christian, What Are the Kids? : A Parenting Guide for Interfaith Families.** New York: UAHC Press, 1993.

Nelson, Rev. Roberta. "Parents as Resident Theologians," in **Religious Education**, vol. 83, no. 4, Fall 1988, pp. 491–497.

Winik, Marion, "Bringing Up Bubba," in **Telling**. New York: Villard/Random House, 1994.

Interfaith Grandparenting

Aldrich, Robert, M.D. and Glenn Austin, M.D., **Grandparenting for the 90s: Parenting is Forever.** Escondido, CA: Robert Erdmann Publishing, Inc., 1991.

LeShan, Eda. **Grandparenting in a Changing World.** New York: Newmarket Press, 1993.

*Levin, Sunie. **Mingled Roots: A Guide for Jewish Grandparents of Interfaith Grandchildren.** Washington, DC: B'nai B'rith Women, 1991.

Children's Questions about God

Boritzer, Etan. **What is God?** Willowdale, Ontario: Firefly Books, 1991.

Gellman, Rabbi Marc, and Monsignor Thomas Hartman. **How Do You Spell God? Answers to the Big Questions from Around the World.** New York: Morrow Junior Books, 1995.

—. **Where Does God Live? Questions and Answers for Parents and Children.** New York: Ballantine Books, 1991.

Groner, Judyth and Madeline Wikler. **Thank You, God! A Jewish child's book of prayers.** Rockville, MD: Kar-Ben Copies, Inc., 1993 (1-800-4-KARBEN).

*Hawxhurst, Joan C. **Bubbe and Gram: My Two Grandmothers.** Kalamazoo, MI: Dovetail Publishing, 1996.

Le Tord, Bijou. **Peace on Earth: A Book of Prayers from Around the World.** New York: Delacorte Press, 1992.

Levine, Deborah J. **Teaching Christian Children about Judaism.** Chicago: Liturgy Training Publications, 1995.

Temple, Tom. **52 Simple Ways to Teach Your Child About God.** Nashville, Tennessee: Oliver-Nelson Books, 1991.

Children's Resources for the Winter Holidays

*Gertz, Susan Enid. **Hanukkah and Christmas at My House.** Middletown, OH: Willow & Laurel Press, 1992.

*Moorman, Margaret. **Light the Lights! A Story about Celebrating Hanukkah & Christmas.** New York: Scholastic Inc., 1994.

O'Keefe, Susan Heyboer. **A Season for Giving.** New York/Mahwah, NJ: Paulist Press, 1990.

Rosen, Michael J. **Elijah's Angel.** New York: Harcourt Brace Jovanovich, 1992.

Sharon, Lois and Bram. **Candles, Snow and Mistletoe.** Drive Entertainment, Inc., 1993 (CD and audiocassette).

Children's Resources for Easter and Passover

Berger, Gilda. **Easter and Other Spring Holidays.** New York: Franklin Watts, 1983.

*Ross, Nancy. **Matzo Bunny.** Litchfield, CT: Powerhouse Advertising & Friends, 1994 (1-860-567-3535).

Silberman, Shoshana. **A Family Haggadah** (vol. I, 1987; vol. II, 1997), and **Songs for a Family Seder** (audiocassette). Rockville, MD: Kar-Ben Copies, Inc. (1-800-4-KARBEN).

We Tell It To Our Children: The Story of Passover. St. Paul, MN: Mensch Makers Press, 1988 (1-612-644-8533).

Resources for Easter and Passover

Klenicki, Rabbi Leon, ed. **The Passover Celebration: A Haggadah for the Seder**, and **Songs for the Seder Meal** (audiocassette). Chicago: Liturgy Training Publications, 1980 (1-800-933-1800).

Saldarini, Anthony J. **Jesus and Passover.** New York: Paulist Press, 1984.

Stallings, Joseph M. **Celebrating an Authentic Passover Seder.** San Jose, CA: Resource Publications, Inc., 1994 (1-800-736-7600).

—. **Rediscovering Passover: A Complete Guide for Christians.** San Jose, California: Resource Publications, Inc., 1995 (revised edition).

Ritual and Prayer in the Home

Imber-Black, Evan and Janine Roberts. **Rituals for Our Times: Celebrating, Healing, and Changing Our Lives and Our Relationships.** New York: HarperCollins, 1992.

Jegen, Carol Frances, BVM, and Rabbi Byron L. Sherwin. **Thank God: Prayers of Jews and Christians Together.** Chicago: Liturgy Training Publications, 1989.

On the Doorposts of Your House: Prayers and Ceremonies for the Jewish Home. New York: CCAR Press, 1994 (1-800-935 CCAR).

Roberts, Elizabeth and Elias Amidon, eds. **Earth Prayers From Around the World.** San Francisco: HarperCollins, 1991.

The Oxford Book of Prayer. New York: Oxford University Press, 1985.

Interfaith Weddings

Brill, Mordecai L., Marlene Halpin, and William H. Genné, eds. **Write Your Own Wedding.** Clinton, NJ: New Win Publishing, 1985.

Diamant, Anita. **The New Jewish Wedding.** New York: Summit Books, 1985.

*Hawxhurst, Joan C. **Interfaith Wedding Ceremonies: Samples and Sources.** Kalamazoo, MI: Dovetail Publishing, 1996.

Klausner, Abraham J. **Weddings: A Complete Guide to All Religious and Interfaith Marriage Services.** Columbus, OH: Alpha Publishing Co., 1986.

Coming-of-Age Ceremonies

Evans, Noela N. **Meditations for the Passages and Celebrations of Life: A Book of Vigils.** Bell Tower, an imprint of Harmony Books, 1995.

Leneman, Cantor Helen. **Bar/Bat Mitzvah Basics: A Practical Guide to Coming of Age Together.** Woodstock, VT: Jewish Lights Publishing, 1996.

Salkin, Rabbi Jeffrey K. **Putting God on the Guest List: How to Reclaim the Spiritual Meaning of Your Child's Bar or Bat Mitzvah.** Woodstock, Vermont: Jewish Lights Publishing, 1992.

Conversion

Berkowitz, Rabbi Allan L. and Patti Moskovitz. **Embracing the Covenant: Converts to Judaism Talk About Why & How.** Woodstock, VT: Jewish Lights Publishing, 1996.

Epstein, Lawrence J. **The Theory and Practice of Welcoming Converts to Judaism.** Lewiston, NY: The Edwin Mellen Press, 1992.

Mayer, Egon, and Amy Avgar. **Conversion Among the Intermarried: Choosing to Become Jewish.** New York: American Jewish Committee, 1987.

Portnoy, Mindy Avra. **Mommy Never Went to Hebrew School.** Rockville, MD: Kar-Ben Copies, 1989.

Romanoff, Lena. **Your People, My People: Finding Acceptance and Fulfillment as a Jew by Choice.** Philadelphia: Jewish Publication Society, 1990.

Death and Mourning

Brener, Anne. **Mourning & Mitzvah: A Guided Journal for Walking the Mourner's Path Through Grief to Healing.** Woodstock, Vermont: Jewish Lights Publishing, 1993.

Childs-Gowell, Elaine. **Good Grief Rituals: Tools for Healing.** Barrytown, NY: Station Hill Press, 1992.

Resources for Interfaith Dialogue and Worship

Fisher, Eugene J. **Faith Without Prejudice.** New York: Crossroad, 1993.

Fisher, Eugene J. and Rabbi Leon Klenicki, eds. **From Desolation to Hope: An Interreligious Holocaust Memorial Service.** New York: Stimulus Foundation, and Chicago: Liturgy Training Publications, 1990.

Fisher, Eugene J. **Homework for Christians: Preparing for Christian-Jewish Dialogue,** and Sternfeld, Janet. **Homework for Jews: Preparing for Jewish-Christian Dialogue.** New York: National Conference of Christians and Jews, 1985.

Fisher, Eugene J., ed. **The Jewish Roots of Christian Liturgy.** Mahwah, NJ: Paulist Press, 1990.

Harrelson, Walter and Randall M. Falk. **Jews & Christians: A Troubled Family.** Nashville: Abingdon Press, 1990.

Klenicki, Rabbi Leon and Reverend Bruce W. Robbins. **Jews and Christians: A Dialogue Service About Prayer.** Chicago: Liturgy Training Publications, 1995.

Pawlikowski, John T. and James T. Wilde. **When Catholics Speak about Jews.** Chicago: Liturgical Training Publications, 1987.

Shermis, Michael and Arthur E. Zannoni. **Introduction to Jewish-Christian Relations.** New York/Mahwah, NJ: Paulist Press, 1991.

Silver, Rabbi Samuel M. **Explaining Judaism to Jews and Christians.** New York: Arco Publishing, 1974.

Zerin, Rabbi Edward. **How to Explain Judaism to Your Non-Jewish Neighbors.** Woodland Hills, CA: Isaac Nathan Publishing, 1997 (818-225-9631).

Historical/Jewish Jesus:

Borg, Marcus J. **Meeting Jesus Again for the First Time: The Historical Jesus & the Heart of Contemporary Faith.** San Francisco: HarperSanFrancisco, 1994.

Borowitz, Eugene. **Contemporary Christologies: A Jewish Response.** New York/Mahwah, NJ: Paulist Press, 1980.

Cox, Harvey. **Many Mansions: A Christian's Encounter with Other Faiths.**
Boston: Beacon Press, 1988.

Crossan, John Dominic. **The Historical Jesus: The Life of a Mediterranean
Jewish Peasant.** San Francisco: HarperSanFrancisco, 1991.

Lapide, Pinchas. **The Resurrection of Jesus: A Jewish Perspective.**
Minneapolis: Augsburg, 1983.

Mitchell, Stephen. **The Gospel According to Jesus: A New Translation
and Guide to his Essential Teachings for Believers and Unbelievers.**
New York: Harper Perennial, 1991.

Neusner, Jacob. **A Rabbi Talks with Jesus.** New York: Doubleday, 1993.

Rahner, Karl, and Pinchas Lapide. **Encountering Jesus—Encountering
Judaism: A Dialogue.** New York: Crossroad, 1987.

Vermes, Geza. **The Religion of Jesus the Jew.** Philadelphia: Fortress, 1993.

Zannoni, Arthur E. **Jews and Christians Speak of Jesus.** Minneapolis:
Fortress Press, 1991.

Other Resources

*An Open Gate: An Exploration of Jewish/Christian Intermarriage.
San Francisco: A Traveling Jewish Theatre, 1992. Audiocassette.

*Dovetail: A Journal by and for Jewish/Christian Families. Bimonthly
periodical available from Dovetail Publishing (1-800-222-0070).

Geffen, Rela Mintz and Egon Mayer. "The Ripple Effect: Interfaith Families
Speak Out." Booklet available from the B'nai B'rith Center for Jewish
Identity (1-202-857-6577).

*Interfaith Ketubah. A six-color interfaith wedding covenant, available
from Good Company in Chicago (1-312-913-9193).

"Interfaith Marriage: A Resource by Presbyterian Christians." Booklet
available from the Presbyterian Church U.S.A. (1-800-524-2612).

Interfaith Resources, Inc. An excellent program designed to promote
discussion between Jews and Christians (1-612-421-1896).

Interfaith Tours. Tours of Israel specially designed for interfaith families
(1-847-251-4889).

Mishpucha et al. Interfaith holiday greeting cards (1-800-764-0953).

MixedBlessing, Inc. Interfaith holiday greeting cards (1-800-947-4004).

Multifaith Calendar, available from Multifaith Resources (1-619-376-4691).

* denotes items of particular interest to or specially recommended for interfaith
families.

Notes

CHAPTER ONE

1. Barry Kosmin and Jeffrey Scheckner, "Highlights of the 1990 National Jewish Population Survey." New York: Council of Jewish Federations, 1991.

2. Jonathan and Judith Pearl, "The Changing Channels of TV's Intermarriage Depictions," in *Dovetail: A Journal by and for Jewish/Christian Families*, June/July 1993, pp. 2–3. For more information on television coverage of Jewish themes, contact the Jewish Televimages Resource Center at (718) 961-1434.

3. "Interfaith Marriage: A Resource by Presbyterian Christians," a booklet produced by the Global Mission Ministry Unit, Office of Ecumenical and Interfaith Relations, Presbyterian Church (U.S.A.). Order through Distribution Management Services (DMS), 100 Witherspoon Street, Louisville, KY 40202-1396, (800) 524-2612.

4. Rabbi Harold Kushner, "Why Do We Need *Dovetail*?," in *Dovetail: A Journal by and for Jewish/Christian Families*, August/September 1992, p. 2.

5. For a complete list of interfaith dialogue and support groups around the nation, see the Bulletin Board section of a recent issue of *Dovetail* (call 800-222-0070 for details on how to obtain a sample issue) or visit Dovetail Publishing's web site at www.mich.com/~dovetail.

CHAPTER TWO

1. Lisa DiCerto Tishler, "Passover Essay," in *America*, April 6, 1991, pp. 380–381.

2. Rabbi Roy Rosenberg, "Can It Be Done? Challenges in Fitting Together Judaism and Christianity," in *Dovetail: A Journal by and for Jewish/Christian Families*, October/November 1992, p. 2.

3. Rabbi Steven Carr Reuben, **Making Interfaith Marriage Work**, Rocklin, CA: Prima Publishing, 1994, p. 221.

CHAPTER THREE

1. For a selection of sample interfaith wedding ceremonies, as well as an extensive resource list, see Joan C. Hawxhurst's **Interfaith Wedding Ceremonies: Samples and Sources**, Kalamazoo, MI: Dovetail Publishing, 1996.

2. For more information on this survey, as well as on an up-to-date list of rabbis willing to officiate at interfaith ceremonies, contact the Rabbinic Center for Research and Counseling, 128 East Dudley Avenue, Westfield, NJ 07090; (908) 233-2288.

CHAPTER FOUR

1. Rev. Dale Hindmarsh et. al., "Jewish-Christian Services: A New Direction," in the National Council of Churches Office of Interfaith Relations' *Lights on Christian-Jewish Relations*, March 1989. For more opinions and guidance on interfaith worship services, see Lawrence A. Hoffman's article, "Jewish-Christian Services—Babel or Mixed Multitude?" in *Cross Currents: Religion & Intellectual Life*, Spring 1990. Rabbi Hoffman, a professor of liturgy at Hebrew Union College in New York, explores what he calls "worship in common" and distinguishes the different types of worship experiences in which Christians and Jews may join together.

2. **Shiron L'Shalom** is published by Jewish Educators for Social Responsibility, 1986.

CHAPTER FIVE

1. Mary Heléne Pottker Rosenbaum and Stanley Ned Rosenbaum, **Celebrating Our Differences: Living Two Faiths in One Marriage**, Shippensburg, PA: Ragged Edge Press, 1994, pp. 165–166.

2. For more information about the Holiday Project in your area, call the National Office at (707) 763-2160.

3. For more details about the evolution of Judaism and Christianity, see Anthony J. Saldarini's **Jesus and Passover**, New York: Paulist Press, 1984.

CHAPTER SIX

1. For summaries of other current research on interfaith couples and their children, see Appendix One.

2. Dr. Glenn Austin, in his answer to a reader's question in *Dovetail: A Journal by and for Jewish/Christian Families*, April/May 1993, pp. 11–12.

3. Juliet Whitcomb, Ph.D. 1996, Adelphi University. For more details of Whitcomb's dissertation research, see her article in *Dovetail: A Journal by and for Jewish/Christian Families*, June/July 1997, pp. 3–4.

4. Barry Kosmin and Jeffrey Scheckner, "Highlights of the 1990 National Jewish Population Survey." New York: Council of Jewish Federations, 1991.

5. From Rabbi Jeffrey K. Salkin's "Children of Interfaith Families in Jewish Religious Schools: An Encounter at the Border," a sermon he gave at the Central Synagogue of Nassau County on December 8, 1995, as reprinted with permission in *Dovetail: A Journal by and for Jewish/Christian Families*, April/May 1996, pp. 3–4.

6. For information on Jewish Renewal in your area, contact Aleph, the Alliance for Jewish Renewal, 7318 Germantown Avenue, Philadelphia, PA 19119-1793, (215) 242-4074.

7. For more information on CLF, write to the Church of the Larger Fellowship, Unitarian Universalist Association, 25 Beacon Street, Boston MA 02108-2823, or call (617) 742-2100. The UUA can also provide you with contact information for Unitarian Universalist congregations in your area.

8. Evan Nelson, Ph.D. 1991, University of North Carolina at Chapel Hill. His dissertation is entitled "The Dynamics of Interfaith Marriage Involving Jews." For more information on Nelson's work, see Appendix One.

CHAPTER SEVEN

1. From "Interfaith Baptism," by the Rev. A.J. Good, in *The Christian Ministry*, November/December 1989, pp. 21–22.

2. Couples who need help in choosing Hebrew, or even English, names for children will find that most rabbis are pretty experienced with this (of course, not all rabbis are sympathetic to interfaith families). For Hebrew names, a good resource is **The New Name Dictionary**, by Alfred J. Kolatch, Jonathan David Publishers, Inc., 68-22 Eliot Avenue, Middle Village, NY 11379.

3. Cantor Leneman's services are available to anyone in the Greater Washington DC area. Contact her at: Cantor Helen Leneman, 10 Defoe Court, Rockville, MD 20850; (301) 762-6682; CantorL@aol.com.

CHAPTER EIGHT

1. Jaida n'ha Sandra, in "How to start a salon (or jump start one)," in *Utne Reader*, July/August 1993, pp. 53–55.

2. All of the groups profiled in this section can be reached by contacting *Dovetail: A Journal by and for Jewish/Christian Families* at 800-222-0070 or dovetail@mich.com.

3. For more information on the Stepping Stones program, contact the Commission on Reform Jewish Outreach, Union of American Hebrew Congregations, 838 Fifth Avenue, New York, NY 10021.

4. For more information on the Pathways program, either in New Jersey or in other parts of the country, call Lynne Wolfe at (201) 884-4800, ext. 192.

5. From Esther Perel's article, "Ethnocultural Factors in Marital Communication Among Intermarried Couples," in the *Journal of Jewish Communal Service*, vol. 66, no. 3, Spring 1990, pp. 244–253.

6. From Rebecca Korzec's article, "A Tale of Two Religions: A Contractual Approach to Religion As a Factor in Child Custody and Visitation Disputes," in the *New England Law Review*, 1991, vol. 25, no. 4, pp. 1121–1136.

7. For more information about the Interfaith Family Mediation Project, contact Rev. Mousin at the Center for Church/State Studies, (312) 362-8673.

Index